Ending with Hope

A RESOURCE FOR CLOSING CONGREGATIONS

Beth Ann Gaede

EDITOR

An Alban Institute Publication

Scripture quotations, unless otherwise noted, are from the New Revised Standard Version of the Bible, copyright © 1989, Division of Christian Education of the National Council of the Churches of Christ in the United States of American, and are used by permission.

Library of Congress Catalog Number 2002104639
ISBN 1-56699263-X

Contents

Preface

Beth Ann Gaede

A group of clergy dawdled over breakfast and second cups of coffee, getting acquainted and telling stories before the start of our daylong meeting. As I listened, I noticed that most of the people at the table had helped to close at least one congregation. I offered my observation to the group and naively asked, "Did you have any resources to help you through the process?" They laughed. And then they explained.

Beyond outlines of judicatory procedures and legal responsibilities, and brief liturgies for a closing worship service, almost no formal resources were available. And even the resources they could locate often failed to provide what congregational leaders and judicatory staff really need to know. For the most part, these pastors noted, what little meaningful help they got came through a sort of underground network. Friends and colleagues, upon hearing what was happening in the struggling congregation, would suggest, "Oh, you should talk to Pastor Miller. She helped her last congregation close, and she might have some ideas."

These pastors went on to describe the denial they have found in the church about the fact that congregations close. They have seen that denial among members of congregations with worship attendance of fewer than a dozen as well as the clergy who serve them. Alban senior consultant Alice Mann offers this account about one 30-year-old congregation.

After ten years, the denomination's mission department realized that early demographic projections had overestimated opportunity in this location; the agency terminated the subsidy with the intention that the congregation would close. How did the church react? "They can't close us!" The congregation vowed to use its own modest resources to keep up the mortgage payments and to employ a pastor, creating a budget that was the institutional equivalent of a starvation diet. One leader spent her time collecting drippings from the altar candles and forming the wax around new strings so that the purchase of candles could be avoided.[1]

Judicatory staff to whom congregations turn for help can be equally blind to reality. One pastor quoted a judicatory leader who announced, "No churches will close on my watch!" Not surprisingly, after his term of office ended, the judicatory experienced a rash of closings among congregations that had been kept on life support until they were finally allowed to die.

"Faith Communities Today," a study recently released by Hartford Seminary, reports that half of all congregations have fewer than 100 regularly participating adults. Mann comments:

> There was a day when a congregation of that size, in many towns and city neighborhoods, could comfortably sustain a building, a full-time pastor, and a modest church program. Today, that is an unlikely scenario. Furthermore, younger generations expect more programs, better quality programs, and more choices about how and when they participate. So even the congregation that can pay for a building and a pastor may find that it cannot meet people's expectations of what a church should offer.[2]

Citing an Evangelical Lutheran Church in America study of ministry in 2000 and the Hartford study, Gilson Waldkoenig, director of the Town and Country Church Institute at the Lutheran Theological Seminary at Gettysburg, has observed, "These pieces add up, in my figuring, to a looming tidal wave of congregational closings for mainline Protestants."[3] Still, denominations generally do not publish statistics about church closings. Those who want to study the trends need to cull through lists of congregations that have merged or disbanded and come up with their own numbers.

It might seem surprising that the Alban Institute would publish a resource about closing congregations. After all, our mission statement says we are "dedicated to encouraging vigorous, faithful congregations by supporting the people of God in ministry within their faith communities and in the world." We believe, however, that although closing a congregation is in many ways about dying, it can also be about new life. The closing of some churches and the movement of those people to both new and established congregations can be a source of revitalization for the receiving congregations. By closing one congregation, energy is released for use in places where God is working in new ways.

At Alban our understanding of the importance of closing churches has grown as we have come to realize what a hard, long process it is to revitalize an established congregation. Indeed, any congregation that hopes to revitalize its ministry would do well to look squarely at the option of closing as well as any other options that have been considered out of bounds. Eventually, as various scenarios are explored, the congregation must ask, "To what ministry is God calling us?" Specifically asking "Why not close?" raises the possibility that God calls some churches to close.

Given that closing a congregation might be consistent with God's call, we at Alban think it is therefore consistent with our own mission to offer a resource that helps congregations, pastors, and judicatory staff address the issues involved in closing congregations. Above all, we hope to help congregational leaders and supporters understand that closing a congregation is not about failure but about redirecting resources for new ministry.

We need to change our attitude toward congregations closing much the way we need to rethink our attitudes toward death. Even medical practitioners are beginning to see that they must change their approach. Jane E. Brody, medical writer for the *New York Times*, has written about the developing understanding that hope plays a role in healing. She cites Dan Shapiro, a clinical psychologist at the University of Arizona School of Medicine: "The medical model says that if you can't cure, you die. A healing model says that even if you can't cure, you can still encourage healing in all phases of life," including bereavement.[4]

Fifteen people have contributed to this volume of healing. Most of them have directly helped congregations through a closing. The others have provided support with other types of ministry. But all of them share the foundational vision for this resource—that closing a congregation is a resurrection opportunity to release resources for new ministry. Part 1 will guide readers as they assess whether it is time for a congregation to close as well as a historical framework for understanding what "closing" might mean to different types of congregations. Further chapters offer reflections about the experience of closing—from the perspective of the pastor, members, congregations considering merger, and judicatory staff. Part 2 includes four case studies written by people who were directly involved in closing a congregation. And part 3 of this book provides resources to help congregational leaders think about what to do with their building and property, how to deal with documents and artifacts, and thoughts about the use of ritual to create a healthy ending.

One pastor in that formative breakfast group, a former bishop's assistant in a rural area, described her experience leading a closing worship service on one of her first Sundays as assistant. Her denomination's rite indicates that at the end of the service, the people "move in procession from the building, taking the worship furnishings and sacramental vessels."[5] As the congregation members carried out these instructions, the bishop's assistant led the procession out onto the prairie. And then she stopped. Now what? What would they do with the Bible, the communionware and the bowl from the baptismal font, the candles sticks and altar book? What next? No one had thought about where the procession would lead, what would happen with these symbols of the congregation's years of faithful ministry.

Ending with Hope: A Resource for Closing Congregations is designed to break the silence about closing congregations and to help congregations think about what they will do when they are standing with the symbols of their ministry—whether on the prairie or the street corner—wondering what comes next. Waldkoening challenges his seminary classes: "Why is it we do funerals so well but often balk at even recognizing the death of a congregation? Couldn't we do grief ministry and funerals as well for social groups as for individuals?"[6] This book provides guidance for those who want to provide the grief ministry congregations need to close well and to move on to new ministry in new places.

Acknowledgments

As editor of this volume, I want to thank the many people who gave so generously of their time, describing their experience in long phone conversations, writing detailed e-mails about the needs of congregations, and in other ways reflecting with me about the important ministry of helping a congregation to close.

Laurie Natwick, now an ELCA pastor in Bismarck, North Dakota, and formerly an assistant to the bishop of western North Dakota, talked with me at length about her experiences with rural parishes and helped me figure out what questions I needed to ask as I looked for contributors to this volume.

Robert Welsh, president of the Council on Christian Unity, generously gave us permission to borrow freely from the resource he developed for the Christian Church (Disciples of Christ), "Is it time to fold the tent? When a ministry shifts elsewhere; how to deal with the pain and process" (Indianapolis, Ind.: Christian Church Foundation, and Board of Church Extension of the Christian Church [Disciples of Christ], undated).

Keith Spencer, one of the contributors to this book, offered me the detailed bibliography he developed and photocopied many pages of resources he uncovered when he wrote about closing churches as part of a seminary course he took with Gilson Waldkoenig, another one of our contributors.

The other contributors to this resource should also be thanked. They are all busy people who made time to write carefully and thoughtfully about their experiences, to recall their own struggles and triumphs, so that others might learn from them. I am grateful to all of them for their hard work.

NOTES

1. Alice Mann, *Can Our Church Live? Redeveloping Congregations in Decline* (Bethesda, Md.: The Alban Institute, 1999), 8.

2. E-mail from Alice Mann to Beth Ann Gaede, February 20, 2002.

3. E-mail from Gilson Waldkoenig to Beth Ann Gaede, May 18, 2001.

4. Jane Brody for the *New York Times,* in "Doctor still has duty if patient dies," Minneapolis *Star Tribune,* May 23, 2001, Metro edition.

5. "Closing of a Congregation," *Occasional Services: Companion to Lutheran Book of Worship* (Minneapolis: Augsburg Publishing House; and Philadelphia: Board of Publication, Lutheran Church in America, 1982), 256–57.

6. E-mail from Gilson Waldkoenig to Beth Ann Gaede, May 18, 2001.

PART 1

Decisions and Dynamics in Closings

1

Discerning God's Calling

Ellen Morseth

Although the word discernment is widely in use today, spiritual discernment remains obscure, mysterious, and even unknown to many people, despite the fact that it is an essential and historic practice of the Christian life. In a nutshell, authentic spiritual discernment is both an individual and a collective habit and practice of prayerfully coming to spiritual insight. It is a developed Christian capacity to discriminate among various options, a gift from God gradually acquired and polished often by the Spirit of God.

People engage in spiritual discernment not to argue for a desired outcome, nor to debate a matter in order to win. We engage in spiritual discernment to prayerfully seek God's yearning in an important matter. The practice of spiritual discernment does not provide a swift, prepackaged solution, nor does it allow for a quick decision among a few good options. It does, however, allow significant time for pondering God's intentions. The practice calls for integrity of heart and mind, and significant time for study and prayer.

Preconditions

Readiness to engage in the practice of spiritual discernment is important because spiritual discernment cannot be "jumped into" as just another way to make a decision. Some preconditions are essential to its practice, so if people cannot agree with the preconditions, another process for making the decision should be determined. Spiritual discernment is not for the faint-hearted, and its practice should not be attempted if people are not sincere about engaging in it. Authentic spiritual discernment calls for walking on holy ground.

Before committing to engage in the practice of spiritual discernment, participants agree to act upon whatever is revealed to them as God's yearning—no matter what the cost, individually or corporately. A significant amount of holy indifference—a radical openness to what God desires—is called for in spiritual discernment. Because God is all-important, the congregation's desires pale in comparison. If this kind of holy indifference is lacking, there is no point in attempting to spiritually discern.

Another precondition for spiritual discernment is the desire and ability to articulate God's presence in the life of the congregation. During the practice of spiritual discernment, faith-filled people whose lives are rooted in prayer and attentive to God's desires for their future will be led into looking beyond their institutional survival. They will find themselves challenged to seek God's larger vision and will pray for God's guidance to move the church forward—by whatever means.

So instead of focusing narrowly on what "I" or "we" want (which we most often do, and which may not encompass the broader picture of a congregation's life), an authentic practice of spiritual discernment will lead a congregation into deep reliance on God as its members share their faith struggles and joys. Just as an individual musician practicing by herself or himself contributes to an orchestra's overall quality, people who personally and communally live and share their faith will provide fertile ground for the practice of spiritual discernment in a congregation.

What Might God Want?

During the 1970s and '80s a virtual explosion of closures, consolidations, and uncomfortable compromises happened in Roman Catholic churches across the United States. This created tensions among bishops, pastors, and church members, and people in rural areas and the inner cities were the most affected. It seemed true then—and does even now—that almost no one was asking the question, "What might God want for this particular congregation with its unique history and identity?" Devastating decisions were made on the basis of financial concerns, limited worship attendance, or the dwindling number of ordained ministers. There seemed to be no available time to consider the affections, associations, and memories that people in these congregations held. These considerations could possibly have provided energy for new directions. But overall, little room was left for the wind of God's Spirit.

There was—and is—a better way to look at a congregation's life and to make a serious decision about its future. I'd like to share with you a story from personal experience that illustrates "a better way." This story points to the fact that we have within our varied faith traditions sacred texts, creeds, stories, and rituals that we often overlook when trying to make important congregational decisions. We also have the ancient practice of spiritual discernment that is new to many faith traditions. My contention is that we really do not need to look to organizational management techniques for process ideas.

In 1984 I was invited by a bishop to assume responsibility as pastoral administrator (a lay person or deacon appointed by a bishop to pastor and administer a parish) of a parish in Montana and its mission church, 35 miles due east. During the course of our conversations, I remember the bishop telling me that the mission church "should have been closed a number of years ago, but no previous pastor had the nerve to do it." Then he told me that he would like me to accomplish this task!

As someone who did not relish being a new pastoral presence with such a goal in mind, I asked the bishop to give me at least three years to assess the situation and to accomplish in some collaborative way an outcome that would be the best decision for everyone involved. Thankfully, he agreed. Then the thought of figuring out how to facilitate significant, prayerful conversations about the life of this long-standing mission church gave me much food for thought and prayer.

My first undertaking over many months was to get to know the people and to be a helpful pastoral presence in their midst. Every Saturday I led their worship service, and before and after the service I engaged in social conversation with whoever was there. Though I intentionally resisted jumping to conclusions about the life of this small congregation, it did not take me long to observe many disturbing facets of their life. For example, the church once having 35 members now had a roster of 12, three to six of whom participated regularly in weekly services. The average weekly stewardship collection was $3.00. And the building, a simple wood structure with no plumbing, desperately needed a new roof. Then, too, I learned that the adults wanted me to provide religious education classes for their children in their town one evening a week, rather than the parents taking some responsibility for bringing their children to already organized classes at the mother church. These parishioners also seemed to think their participation in adult education events and retreats was totally out of the question.

My overall discovery was that for the majority of parishioners, "church" meant a building of convenience. And my ministry was taken for granted. This small community seemed unwilling—and in some cases the people were just not able—to take responsibility for their own religious growth, for stewardship of the building and land, and for a relationship with the larger diocesan faith community.

After one year as their minister, my attempts to initiate conversations about ongoing formation for ministry, stewardship, and a relationship to the larger diocese seemed to have fallen on deaf ears. This congregation's life appeared to be stuck in neutral gear, and I was becoming more convinced that some decision about its life had to be made—and owned—by the people involved. But I had no positive case studies to guide me on the ways of closing or merging Catholic parishes.

After much thought and prayer about this situation, I became inspired to use the three-year cycle of Sunday lectionary readings as the focus for spiritual discernment via communal storytelling and reflection on the life of this mission church. This took place from 1985 to 1987—literally evolving week by week—without a strategic plan. I invited stories about the history of the small town and how the church came to be. We looked at the data from old newspapers collected in the diocesan archives, and one of the "oldtimers" shared some photographs from horse and buggy days. The parishioners talked about the good times as well as their families' lives during the depression. Through all the storytelling, I was trying to help all of us see the big picture up until now.

I very specifically engaged the parishioners in reflection on the story of their church via homilies, meetings after our worship time, and prayers of intercession that named our dilemmas and asked for God's continued guidance. I noted in the gospel stories such things as opportunities, crisis events, or people taking risks, and then invited the parishioners to name and describe an event in their parish life that had some of the same elements. I engaged them in these conversations because by now I was very conscious of the fact that they had great difficulty connecting their little church life to the larger church beyond themselves.

Our conversations slowly began to surface some hopes the parishioners harbored about the church's viability, such as their expectation that they would always be taken care of regardless of their investment in the church. The conversations also uncovered some myths that had lingered on in their collective memory for years. If, in fact, some aspects of these myths were true, whatever truth they had once contained was no longer visible.

During Advent we talked more in depth about the birth of this faith community. Then we moved on to tell about some Epiphany moments in its history (the eventual purchase of stained-glass windows, for example). During Ordinary Time, we talked about the years of seeming stability, acknowledging how the church even contributed to the town's growth. During Lent we reflected seriously on the mystery of death, on what it means to personally die to our own desires for the sake of the common good. During Easter and Pentecost we spoke of rising to new life in Jesus Christ and our need to rely on God's spirit for sustenance and direction.

Gradually unspoken feelings of anger and betrayal (generally focused on the diocese, the bishop, and me for calling their parish life into question) began to surface. However, I still found the lectionary most helpful as a common focus, because we were using what was deeply intrinsic to our worship life—not a process that called for debate or invited hidden agendas—to construct our conversations and move us forward toward some decision about the church's future.

During the second Lenten season, the parishioners came to name and claim the decline of their church as their own responsibility. The oldest member even said publicly, "Sister, you're not to blame for this situation. We've known this was coming." That was a poignant moment. Her naming of the reality made it all okay—not pleasant, not welcome, but okay. Now this small group of parishioners could begin to let go of the past and take hold of their present situation.

The decision that this mission church needed to close was made by the parishioners one Saturday evening, but the process of spiritual discernment was far from over. The few active parishioners who wanted to continue as members of a parish needed to be able to call some parish "home." So I initiated conversations with the councils of both neighboring parishes—35 miles east and 35 miles west. (Meetings and bulletin inserts had already been used to keep their members informed of the evolving situation at the mission church.) The faith community at the mother church (where I ministered) was more understanding of the situation than the other community, which was less able to put itself in the others' shoes.

The last worship service at the mission church was on Good Friday. Following the prescribed ritual and then a period of tearful silence, we removed the tabernacle, crucifix, lectern, altar, and then the cross that hung on the outside of the building. The altar stone was removed (as is customary; it is archived at the mother church), and the altar was dismantled, then buried. Then the doors of the church were closed and locked. As the ritual concluded, those present announced the name of the parish they would be joining on Easter Sunday.

On Easter Sunday, a few small sacred items from the former mission church were carried in procession into the two houses of worship,[1] and following the liturgy, every new member was personally welcomed at receptions in the parish halls.

This is indeed a sacred story, a story of life, decline, death, and new life. It is a story of denial, anger, great grief, closure, and eventual rebirth. The Word of God, opened and shared, helped reveal God's plan for this small congregation. Whether faith communities in the 21st century deny the reality of their life together or actively grapple with what God's intentions might be for their future, it is quite possible that the church's lectionary readings can provide an appropriate and challenging means—as well as spiritual energy—to help parishioners face their future together.

The Movements of Spiritual Discernment

Henri Nouwen wrote in his book *Life of the Beloved: Spiritual Living in a Secular World*, "The movement of God's Spirit is very gentle, very soft. . . . But that movement is also very persistent, strong, and deep. It changes hearts radically."[2] This is a good description of what happens when people become engaged in the "movements" of spiritual discernment, which are described in detail in *Discerning God's Will Together: A Spiritual Practice for the Church* by Charles M. Olsen and Danny E. Morris. This resource and my own book, *Ritual and the Arts in Spiritual Discernment*, offer quite thorough explanations of the movements—which are not lockstep stages in an airtight process. The content of these books helps readers imagine how radical change can happen when rational thought is accompanied by biblical and theological reflection and engagement in the arts during authentic spiritual discernment.

Because members of the small Montana congregation would not have understood the language of spiritual discernment, I did not specifically name the movements as they were experiencing them. But let me now make these connections for you.

The movements begin with framing and conclude with resting, and there is great fluidity within and between these movements. In fact, it is desirable to give as much prayer, conversation, research, and spiritual care as needed to each of the movements.

Framing

During the framing movement, we formulate a question addressed to God. A small group, perhaps the board or pastoral staff, may work to frame the question before proposing it to the congregation (where it may be refined). What is the congregation asking of God? For example, "God, is it your yearning that . . . ?" or "God, what is your preferred future for . . . ?" For the Montana congregation the question was God, what is your desire for our future?

Coming to the right question may take longer than one might think, but the time is well spent because it is important that the question be succinct and clear, so that everyone understands it. Yet, be aware that if the question is not framed as a question asked of God, the question will be talked about—and probably answered—in terms of our own desire, as good as our intention might be. Returning again and again to the God question keeps us centered on God's desire.

Grounding

The church board and pastoral staff might also want to pursue the grounding movement, at least in order to suggest a "guiding principle" for consideration by the congregation at large. A guiding principle is something that is so important to the life of the congregation that it is nonnegotiable. A guiding principle sets boundaries, is informed by the community's values, and therefore may be part of a congregation's mission or vision statement, unless the statement is outdated or too generic. Eventually every option surfaced during the discernment process will be judged via the guiding principle.

It was difficult for the parishioners in the Montana church to come to agreement on a guiding principle. Two people (and I) thought it should reflect the founding story, the importance of being about ministry and being in relationship to the larger diocese. Because there was controversy surrounding the formation of a guiding principle, we chose a more generic one: "God's yearning." This would suffice in our situation.

After the framed question and guiding principle have been worked on by the board, staff, or other small group, the entire congregation is in conversation until everyone eventually agrees on the God question and the guiding principle.

Rooting and Shedding

The rooting and shedding movements in spiritual discernment are shaped
by the framed question and the guiding principle. Rooting involves telling
stories from Scripture, from the denomination's tradition, and about the
particular congregation that will inform the question being asked of God. A
time of rooting in tradition is meant to help the group form a "corporate
memory"[3] or "get on the same page" with their history. There seems to be
a general myth in congregations that "everyone knows the story," which
generally is not true. "Everyone has a piece of the story"[4]—even if it is a
story about what happened at church last Sunday.

The rooting movement proved to be an eye-opening experience for
the Montana congregation. They discovered how much hard work went
into the founding of their church—not only the physical labor of constructing
and maintaining the building and grounds, but the spiritual energy that went
into securing missionaries for periodic liturgical services. Then, too, the
early parishioners worked hard at sustaining their spiritual lives by ministering
to each other during times of great hardship.

Storytelling in spiritual discernment calls for putting all the pieces of
the story together, so that everyone knows the "thicker" story. It is then
that biblical and theological reflection on the story can help the congregation
understand itself—its priorities and values. When we wove the Montana
congregation's story with the scripture stories of the lectionary, the
parishioners began to see that they were not living out of their founding
story. They had let go of some enthusiasm for a spiritual life together. Their
values were focused on themselves. As we reflected on Luke 4:16-21,
they saw that they were not open to concern for the poor, the stranger, the
unwanted, and the marginalized of society as an integral part of living out
the mission of Jesus.

The shedding movement is to be engaged in throughout a process of
spiritual discernment. Even though we struggle individually and collectively
to let go of our own desires, it seems that our egos still get in the way—
even after we have agreed on the preconditions, desire God's yearning in
the matter, and attempt to follow what seems to be God's yearning before
we are certain what that yearning is. Shedding is a time of coming to a holy
indifference about anything other than God's yearning. It is a time of dealing
with hard facts about oneself and about the congregation at large.

When challenged to let go of or release some of their own desires and
fears, the congregation in Montana found it much more comfortable to be

quietly introspective, or to retort by placing blame for the church's decline elsewhere. It is difficult to confront and name what needs to die in us so that we might allow God the room to do something new. Thus, it was important to me that I not rush the pace of their shedding. It was slow, like life naturally is in rural communities.

For quite a long time, the parishioners avoided talking about the present and attempted to keep on living in the "glory days" of the past. But eventually time caught up. Maybe, as Bonhoeffer suggests, the community of Christ can only really be formed when some of its hopes and dreams have been shattered.

Another way to visualize the movements of spiritual discernment is to relate them to the practice of planting, maturing, and harvesting seeds. The framing movement can be thought of as "selecting the seed." The movements of grounding, rooting, and shedding are clustered together as "preparing the soil." The following cluster of movements—listening, exploring, and improving—are about "cultivating the plants."[5]

Listening

The listening movement does not happen just once but is threaded throughout spiritual discernment. Its purpose is to give attentive consideration to every voice that needs to be heard—the voices both within and outside the congregation who will be affected by the ultimate decision, the voices the congregation does not want to listen to, the voice of Scripture, the voice of God's Spirit that can be heard within and in between spoken words, the unspoken words or resistance, and the feelings that accompany all the words. Listening in spiritual discernment is a very intentional effort to collect wisdom that comes in both subjective and objective ways.

A tendency in some congregations is to listen only to the opinions of certain members and to ignore the opinions of others. This type of selective hearing has no place in spiritual discernment, even though it may be quite difficult to encourage parishioners to stretch themselves beyond their usual modes of behavior. The Montana parishioners really did not want to listen to me or to their bishop for a while. When this kind of resistance is present, a good measure of God's grace is required on the part of church leaders to allow more time for listening. God's Spirit will break through.

Exploring

During the exploring movement, the congregation looks at every possible option for God's preferred future through the lens of their guiding principle. This movement calls for dreaming and visioning beyond what may be seen as the only "practical" solution. Maybe some never-before-imagined possibilities will emerge from the thought and prayer given to this movement. The congregation might ask itself such questions as: "What creative structures or relationships exist in churches of other denominations?" or "If we had no financial constraints, what might God want to happen here?" The exploring movement is an opportunity to think outside the proverbial box.

The Montana congregation explored two options: closing its doors or merging with either of the other congregations 35 miles to the west or to the east of it. (The locale, the small number of members, and some apathy all contributed to the lack of other options.)

Improving

Once options are discovered and named, the congregation engages in the improving movement, working with each option until it becomes the best that it can be. For example, a component might be added to an option, or a section of an option might be refined. No option is given lesser consideration; each option is considered as if it might be the one option God desires for the congregation.

Another look at the congregation's story with its particular history, values, and traditions may be helpful during this improving movement. Certainly, looking at each option alongside the guiding principle is essential; the guiding principle is not a lens that should gather dust.

When the Montana congregation engaged in "improving" the two options they were considering, they discovered a third option: close the church building and invite each parishioner to choose which one of the other two churches to join. (There were no local ecumenical options; their church was the only one in town.)

Weighing

Once each option is refined to the best that it can be, it is time to enter into the weighing movement. Each option is then carefully and prayerfully weighed. What is the driving force behind each option? Is it the Spirit of God, or some lesser spirit? Does one option seem preferable because it is less costly (in financial or human resource terms)?

More than human judgment is involved in weighing. John Cassian, a fourth-century church father and the writer of *Conferences*, offers a five-way test that remains helpful:

1. Is it filled with what is good for all?
2. Is it heavy with the fear of God?
3. Is it genuine in the feelings that underlie it?
4. Is it lightweight because of human show or because of some thrust toward novelty?
5. Has the burden of vainglory lessened its merit or diminished its luster?[6]

The option of closing the doors on the Montana church and walking away did not seem to the parishioners to be "filled with what is good for all." Merging as a group with either of the other two churches was a possibility, and the third option of inviting each parishioner to choose which church to join also seemed to be a viable option. Once the parishioners talked and prayed more about those two options, it was time to come to some closure.

Closing

During the closing movement in spiritual discernment, a congregation decides which option seems to be that for which God most yearns. The option may be welcome or unwelcome, but the decision is made by walking in faith, not just with human sight. The congregation and its leaders continue their prayerful work in concert with God—to uncover what God is calling the congregation to be in the future.

A process of spiritually discerning the congregation's future began by framing a question to God. When we began to reach closure, the congregation worked on its response to God by stating: "God, it seems to us that your yearning is . . ."

The congregation in Montana prayerfully closed on the third option: closing the church and inviting each parishioner to choose which other church to join. Acting on this option would be difficult, but it also seemed to them to be the most spiritually life-giving.

Resting

Spiritual discernment, however, is never concluded during the closing movement. By resting with the decision (which is not yet added to council minutes or written in gold), the congregation and its leaders give the decision the "test of the heart."

Ignatian discernment, which derives from Ignatius of Loyola, the founder of the Jesuit Order in 1540 and author of *The Spiritual Exercises*, invites us to give the selected option a test of the heart. In other words, is there *consolation*—a sense of peace and movement toward God, even if the decision is a difficult one, or *desolation*—a sense of discomfort and movement away from God; a feeling that God may want something more, or something else—with the option? Because collaboration with God for the well-being of the human family is at stake, this resting movement, as all other movements, should not be rushed, but allowed some quality time.

As you have already learned, the Montana congregation ritualized, in very significant ways during the seasons of Lent and Easter, its own coming to rest on a very difficult decision. That decision still seems to have been God's yearning.

Conclusion

In its search for spiritual meaning and for spiritual hope, a congregation can, over time, come to be at peace with the pain of closing or merging or linking or yoking. During a process of spiritual discernment, a congregation may discover new ways of living together, bringing new life into its communal soul. It may discover a capacity for self-transcendence. It may uncover its myths or its own inability to see God's bigger picture. In any scenario, whatever is uncovered has the potential of being a gift to the congregation from God's Spirit.

The age-old practice of spiritual discernment, as well as the liturgical seasons of the church year, offer process possibilities to the church. By incorporating these into our decision making, we will surely be challenged to be thoughtful, prayerful, honest, and strong, and to let God's Spirit do its work. As God's people, we can spiritually discern—and spiritual discernment will illumine, clarify, and strengthen what we already believe we know through human reason.

NOTES

1. The church building was sold to a trucking company (for a storage facility) a few months later.

2. Henri Nouwen, *Life of the Beloved: Spiritual Living in a Secular World* (New York: Crossroad, 1997), 63.

3. Charles M. Olsen, *Transforming Church Boards into Communities of Spiritual Leaders* (Bethesda, Md.: The Alban Institute, 1995), 70.

4. Mary Benet McKinney, *Sharing Wisdom: A Process for Group Decision Making* (Valencia, Calif.: Tabor Publishing, 1987), 13.

5. Danny E. Morris and Charles M. Olsen, *Discerning God's Will Together: A Spiritual Practice for the Church* (Bethesda, Md.: The Alban Institute, 1997), 92–93.

6. John Cassian, *Conferences* 1:21 (New York: Paulist Press, 1985), 57.

2

Assessing Congregational Viability

Keith Spencer

St. Timothy Lutheran Church, founded by farming families over a century ago, is facing a crisis. For generations farm families had filled its pews, enjoyed potlucks and holidays there, and watched their children move up from classroom to classroom in its Sunday school. Within one generation, however, most of the community's children left the farms for new careers in other places. Farm after farm was sold to developers eager to transform the verdant landscape into bedroom communities for the burgeoning city an hour's commute to the south. Members still brought in jars of honey, vegetables, and meat in season for the part-time pastor and seminary student assistant, but the harvests were in decline as was St. Timothy's membership. In 1997 it listed 161 baptized members and an average worship attendance of 58. As older members have died and their children and grandchildren have found churches closer to their homes, members of St. Timothy have come to realize that if they do not take significant steps, it is unlikely that the decline will be reversed. It is their church, and it is dying. But no one talks about it.

Grace Church, founded by immigrants who arrived in the sprawling city in waves before the First World War, has been in decline like the city around it for the past three decades. A social service agency and its child care program now occupy the second floor of its Sunday school building, which once could not contain the many children who filled its rooms and even its hallways each Sunday. The folding chairs that had supplemented the polished wooden pews during worship, especially at the holidays, are rusting on their carts. Throngs of people no longer walk from their nearby row houses and gather for coffee in its fellowship hall or chat in the parlor before worship. What remains of the congregation's savings dwindles year after year. Internal conflict and tumultuous relationships among the members, its leaders, and several of its pastors have taken their toll as well. First, the congregation could no longer afford a full-time pastor and then had difficulty affording a part-time pastor. In the neighborhood, a rebirth has begun, yet few new families seem to visit more than once. At the early service fewer than two dozen members are widely dispersed among the empty pews. For a while no one spoke the words out loud, until finally those who remained admitted to themselves that a crisis is at hand. The leaders have met with denominational representatives and other churches willing to help. They have come together to discuss one question: Are we still a viable congregation?

Holy Trinity Church had nearly 200 members in worship only a few years ago but now sees perhaps three dozen or so each Sunday, with more on the holidays. Founded during the post–World War II boom of the 1950s, it enjoyed health for many years. The congregation opened its building for a weekly soup kitchen, but in recent years that ministry has given way to a food pantry that members now struggle to keep reasonably stocked. The neighborhood, once a sprawling, all-white, post-war suburb, now boasts an ethnic diversity to rival any city in America. The main-street church finds itself surrounded by used car dealerships, pawn shops, payday loan establishments, and adult bookstores. Served by a part-time interim pastor, the members who remain, mostly seniors well into their seventh or later decade of life, continue to keep up the property as best they can, renting their facilities to another congregation and other groups to supplement their shrinking income. An attempt a few years ago to discuss the congregation's future with denominational leaders and nearby parishes ended with hurt feelings and mistrust. The church leaders walked away believing that neighboring churches and denominational leadership wanted nothing more than to shut down the congregation and reap the benefits of selling off its assets. They cling to the hope that the projected future regeneration of the main street and its surrounding neighborhood will bring them along with it. For now, they just survive.

Sunday school classrooms are gathering dust. The voices of children have been long absent during worship. Cry rooms and nurseries have become storage closets. The visitor book gathers names primarily at Christmas and Easter. The treasurer's report each month brings the grim realities that expenses exceed income and bills cannot be paid. In the Evangelical Lutheran Church in America, the largest Lutheran denomination in America, one study showed that from 1996 to 2000 over 41 percent of its congregations

declined more than 5 percent in average Sunday worship attendance.[1] The
sad thing is that this statistic will not surprise many of us. We have been to
these churches. We call them home.

What Is God Calling Us to Do in This Place?

In many communities, our homes and churches are at risk, and it is time for
us to ask ourselves a question of great significance: What is God calling us
to do in this place? It is the core question for ministry. During the birth or
rebirth of a congregation, this question can anchor us with a growing sense
of hope and joy and promise. It is just as likely, however, that congregations
turn to this basic question at a time of crisis: the arrival of a new pastor or
other significant change in congregational leadership, a major change in the
availability or condition of facilities, a financial windfall or shortfall, or when
congregational viability seems to be threatened.

Discerning what God is calling us to do as a congregation might appear
on the surface to have little to do with congregational viability. Surely, God
calls us to the work of the Gospel: to preach, teach, baptize, to go make
disciples. The words "congregational viability" seem cold and scientific.
We do not want to talk about the viability of our congregation; rather, we
want to share its faith stories and its hopes. We want to recount stories
about the children at the font, the couples at the chancel, the suppers,
Christmases, and Easters. Unfortunately, too many congregations put off
conversations about viability until there are no longer choices to be made.
They use silence as an escape from growing fears that the congregation
may be dying. Silently, they hope that the congregation will last long enough
for those who remain to move on or to be buried, and for the last grandchild
to be baptized or perhaps married.

Closure Is Not Failure

Eventually, however, we must face the question: What is God calling us to
do in this place? But how that discussion is framed—what is on the table
and what is off—will have a significant impact on the answer we hear.
One pastor of a struggling church lamented how much more difficult the
discussion of viability became as his congregation held firmly onto the belief

that closure was failure, effectively moving the option of closure off the table. Members of that congregation confused a church with the church universal. The pastor of the church in our third opening example, believing that the denomination and his fellow neighborhood pastors wanted his parish to close so they could divide up "the spoils," vowed that his parish "would never close!" A rallying cry of defense during an emotional meeting, his words affirmed to a degree the understanding that church closure equals church failure. The belief that churches are not supposed to close, ever, is found not only among pastors and congregations, but also among denominational officials. During a study on church closure, one Lutheran bishop shared how no congregation had closed during his tenure, but several were "holding on by their fingertips." Is it possible that some of these congregations continued to remain open only because they had never been permitted to discuss closure?

A Healthy Understanding of a Church's Life

Congregations that understand the life cycle of churches are more likely to engage in discussion about the possibility of closure. So what might a healthy understanding of the life cycle of a church look like? How does a church differ from the church universal?

Individual congregations are not immortal. Further, like individuals, congregations are born, grow, may get sick, can recover, will age, and will eventually die. Death may come unexpectedly and suddenly. Death may come slowly after a long period of illness. But death will come. Like a few people (remember those hundred-plus-year-old residents of the former Georgian Soviet Socialist Republic a few years back used to promote a brand of American yogurt?), some churches may live for many, many years. In those cases, churches may seem more like Galapagos tortoises, or even giant redwoods, than human beings. But tortoises and even redwoods eventually die. Death is a natural event. Our body's design causes it to yield in time to the forces of aging—despite exercise, vitamins, or the most severe health regimen. Like us, congregations are not immortal. Eventually, when the money runs out or the core leaders pass away or the work just plain exhausts them, they will fail. Of course, as Elizabeth Kübler-Ross noted in her seminal work on death and dying, denial is the first stage of one journey's when facing death. Let's face it: given the choice between the fantasy of immortality and the grim reality of dying and death, the fantasy will win almost every time. Congregations are not immune to corporate denial.

Understanding that a healthy discussion of viability must include the option of closure, how might a congregation, its leaders, or a committee or group approach such a discussion? What tools or assessments are available? What questions should be asked? What information should be provided to the participants? It is to these questions that we now turn.

Discernment

The starting point for discernment is prayer. The leaders of the congregation and the congregation itself can center on this prayer, surround themselves with it: What is God calling us to do in this place? They can print it in 14-point bold type in the bulletins and splash it below the masthead in the newsletter. The can paint it on sheets or sew it in felt letters on banners and hang it in the sanctuary and fellowship hall. Pastors should preach on it. Parishioners should pour the coffee, pull up some chairs, and chat about it over cake and pie. Members should take the prayer home with them, tape it to the bathroom mirror, and pray it daily, honestly, and continuously. Finally, as the congregation's leaders gather to take action, they can write it on the chalkboard, on the flipchart, on the tops of yellow legal pads—keep it ever before them. What is God calling us to do in this place?

Once a congregation is centered in this prayer, then what? A good next step is for the congregational leaders to examine what your denomination's faith documents and constitution, if your denomination has them, say about a viable congregation. For example, the Evangelical Lutheran Church in America's constitution states:

> A Congregation is a community of baptized persons whose existence depends upon the proclamation of the Gospel and the administration of the sacraments whose purpose is to worship God, to nurture its members, and to reach out in witness and service to the world. To this end it assembles regularly for worship and nurture, organizes and carries out its ministry to its people and neighborhood, and cooperates with and supports the wider church to strive for the fulfillment of God's mission in the world.[2]

From this document we could derive that a viable congregation:

1. meets regularly for worship centered on Word and Sacrament and spiritual nurture
2. reaches out to both its members and the community
3. cooperates with and supports the ministry of the wider church for the fulfillment of God's mission in the world

Similarly, the Presbyterian Church (U.S.A.) in its Book of Order declares that the church is called to be Christ's faithful evangelist by

1. going into the world, making disciples of all nations, baptizing them in the name of the Father and of the Son and of the Holy Spirit, teaching them to observe all he has commanded
2. demonstrating by the love of its members for one another and by the quality of its common life the new reality in Christ; sharing in worship, fellowship, and nurture; practicing a deepened life of prayer and service under the guidance of the Holy Spirit
3. participating in God's activity in the world through its life for others by healing and reconciling and binding up wounds; ministering to the needs of the poor, the sick, the lonely, and the powerless; engaging in the struggle to free people from sin, fear, oppression, hunger, and injustice; giving itself and its substance to the service of those who suffer; sharing with Christ in the establishing of his just, peaceable, and loving rule in the world.[3]

Such tools might be used in a small-group discussion-and-report format. Members of the board and other key leaders break into small groups, each focusing on an area of congregational activity identified in the key documents. Using the PCUSA example, three groups each take one activity—"going," "demonstrating," or "participating"—and spend sufficient time, perhaps 45 minutes or so, reflecting on (1) how the congregation lives out the activity, (2) what barriers may prevent fulfilling the congregational activity, and (3) ways in which these barriers might be overcome. After the small-group discussion period, each group then summarizes its discussion for the whole assembly.

Next, the whole group might consider the suggestions for overcoming barriers. Will they be sufficient to meet the challenge? Does the congregation have the resources (or have access to them through other churches, denominational offices, or others) to put these suggestions into practice? Does the congregation have the will and desire to do what it takes to carry out these actions? Note those areas where difficulties in overcoming barriers may exist. Careful note taking to summarize the work of the small groups and their presentations and the general discussion of the whole group is essential.

The Classification System Approach

Although statistics do not and cannot tell the whole story, they can be useful tools for evaluating viability. One such tool that has been employed by some denominational staffs is called the Classification System Approach.[4] With this approach congregations are classified in terms of their mission status. Data for classification come from a variety of sources, with denominational staffs providing significant input.

One such example of a classification system includes five categories:

1. resource congregations
2. strong congregations
3. stable congregations
4. challenge congregations
5. at-risk congregations

This system uses the following criteria to define at-risk congregations:

*   insufficient numbers of persons to maintain critical mass for volunteer ministry and financial support
*   barely able or unable to sustain full-time pastoral ministry
*   average worship attendance less than 50
*   survival goals predominate
*   lack of clear parish boundaries

The strengths of this approach include:

*   its proactive nature and its ability to identify both at-risk congregations and possible congregational partners who evolve into resource partners

- its capacity to open the door for intervention and assistance; for example, trained teams that visit at-risk congregations to partner with them early on in the process of viability assessment

The major weakness is that categories may be perceived as labels that might positively or negatively affect perceptions both within and outside of the congregation. Such labels could interfere with the intent: to identify congregations at risk and in need of help, and those congregations that may have the gifts and resources to help them.

Given the reluctance of both congregations and denominations to deal with the closing of congregations, it is not surprising that few resources have been developed to address the matter. One courageous denomination, the Christian Church (Disciples of Christ), however, has been bold enough to prepare a fine publication about the issue, "Is it time to fold the tent?"[5] Much of what follows is borrowed from that piece, with the denomination's permission.

Taking a Survey

An alternative to the small-group discussion-and-report format is taking a congregational survey whose data would then form the basis of a discussion among the leaders. For example, the following survey could be used to evaluate five indicators of a congregation's viability:

Please indicate the degree to which you believe that the following descriptions reflect the situation in your congregation by writing "very much," "somewhat," or "not at all."

_____	1. Total concentration on member-oriented activities
_____	2. Excessive emphasis on the past
_____	3. A neighborhood church without a neighborhood constituency
_____	4. A rebellion against denominational requests for financial support
_____	5. A firm resistance to change

Space may be added after each question or at the end of the survey for additional comments.

This survey lists five of the warning signs enumerated by parish consultant Lyle Schaller that will assist in the discussion of viability in your congregation's current context:

1. **Total concentration on member-oriented activities.** When the congregation lapses into a survival mode, caring only for its well-being and providing resources only for its own programming, we see a telltale sign that the church is in trouble.
2. **Excessive emphasis on the past.** Although pride in past achievement is good, obsession with looking back creates a pillar of salt that says the present and the future are being neglected.
3. **A neighborhood church without a neighborhood constituency.** By nature, the church is an integral part of the community. If a large majority of the members of a congregation have to leave their neighborhoods to attend church, this is often a sign of impending decline.
4. **A rebellion against denominational requests for financial support.** Although congregations will not always be happy with the way their denomination works, failure to support the wider work, says Schaller, is a sign of trouble.
5. **A firm resistance to change.** Being "set in one's way" is a warning of creeping obsolescence for churches, as well as people and machinery.

Taking the Next Step

Having conducted preliminary work, it should now be clearer if conditions warrant continuing your discernment about your congregation's viability. There is no "score" involved here. The methods are meant to help discern areas of concern. If after your initial period of prayer, investigation, discussion, and reflection several areas of concern are raised, then a more thorough process is recommended to continue your discernment.

Seek Counsel

Many churches have denominational resources and staff who can assist churches as they consider viability and the possibility of closure. Some denominations, in fact, mandate denominational or judicatory participation in the process—if not outright control of it. So the first step is to seek counsel. Staff members may provide input on demographics, the status of other churches in the area, and creative possibilities for cooperative ministry, and discuss legal issues on property, buildings, and a myriad of other issues.

Contacting denominational staff is the last thing some churches want to do. Some react this way reflexively because of issues having to do with control, past history, strained relationships, or assumptions that they have made. A story is told of an assistant to a Lutheran bishop in the Midwest who some years ago earned the reputation as the bishop's hatchet man because he was involved in so many church closures. Every time he was seen, pastors and their churches would go into hiding and lock the door. Such tales become part of church folklore and take on a life of their own and often generate unwarranted fear that renders a congregation unwilling to seek counsel at a time when it needs every bit of help it can find. Congregations should not let the process of discerning what God is calling them to do become captive to fear. When they feel fear and mistrust taking over, it is time to slow down, pray, reflect on what is behind that fear and mistrust, consider what would be lost by giving them up, and perhaps to seek outside counsel.

Form an Evaluation Committee

The second step is for the congregation to form an evaluation committee. Regardless of what group or committee participated in the initial discussion, this committee needs to be composed of the most trusted and gifted leaders. It is the single most important committee a church will ever form. Leaders must be willing to reflect dispassionately on the information and issues, and to make hard decisions that will ultimately face scrutiny by their fellow parishioners and denominational staff.

More Intensive Research and Reflection

Third, the committee needs to set about the task of studying the church's viability in greater depth. The following seven questions could form the basis for such a study:

1. Has the congregation experienced a long-term and continuing decline in its membership and attendance at worship services?
Congregations should compile statistics from at least the past 10 years. Denominational staff may be able to assist in providing the needed data from their records. Often, when a congregation has experienced a significant decline, accurate record keeping becomes a casuality. In that case, members should compile the data to the best of their ability.

2. What is the predominant age group of the congregation?
Develop two forms, one for total membership and one for actively participating members, dividing each group into male and female. Then determine how many people of each age group (70 and above, 60–69, 50–59, 49–40, 39–30, and under 20) the congregation has. Once the data are determined, the question needs to be raised: How many of those who are members are prevented by age or infirmity from participating in the work and witness of the congregation?

3. Has the congregation maintained a good level of stewardship?
Look for data that will indicate the ratio of money spent on strictly local purposes (building maintenance, salaries, and so forth) compared with the amount invested in mission efforts locally and worldwide. Generally, a good investment in outreach is a healthy sign. Can the congregation afford to pay a pastor? What is the stewardship potential of the congregation as it now exists?

4. Has the community in which the congregation is located changed radically since the congregation reached its membership peak?
This information may be available through your denominational staff, the U.S. Census Bureau, or through professional demographic services for a fee. A shifting population pattern from one racial-ethnic or economic group to another presents one set of issues. The change from a residential to a business or industrial community presents another challenge.

5. Is the congregation willing or able to adapt its ministry and lifestyle in order to develop the ministries that will meet the needs of a changed community?
If there is a change in the community, ask the members about their willingness to embrace multiethnic or multilingual ministries. Is the congregation open to hosting a racially ethnic congregation? Can the congregation provide special ministries or services to workers or to businesses if a change to industry or business is the transition issue?

6. Is the present facility physically adaptable for use? Is it in need of repairs?
Is the building accessible for all people or can it be made accessible? Can parts of the building be shut off? Are the utilities affordable? Are major repairs needed? Are the resources available for the repairs? Are the facilities in violation of local codes or are they unsafe?

7. Are new efforts in evangelism and education feasible?
Are there unchurched people in the local community, and does the congregation have the leadership, passion, and resources to reach out to them and provide for their education in the faith? List the resources of church members, and evaluate whether there are sufficient funds and will to conduct an adequate program to reach out to those without a church connection.

Considering the Options

At least five options should be considered following the more intensive study of ministry viability:

1. Continue the present ministry in the present location.
The caveat here is that the congregation must continuously monitor the situation, so that it does not continue its ministry while declining to the point that responsible decisions about the future cannot be made. Tough decision making about congregational viability means looking at key elements, such as the ability to provide for a pastor, to maintain facilities, and to accomplish ministry of the gospel.

2.   Arrange to share facilities with another congregation.
Although this option relieves one congregation of the burden of maintaining its own property and could provide much-needed capital, leaving one's own church building could carry significant emotional trauma. Sharing facilities requires patience, understanding, clearly defined responsibilities and expectations, and a sense of service to the greater mission of the church in the world.

3.   Relocate to a growing area of the community.
This option requires careful coordination with denominational staff and significant preliminary research. It is a difficult choice for a congregation without a clear vision of new ministry for the new area, adequate financial resources, and large amounts of congregational energy. A move alone will not typically turn around a congregation without a fresh vision, energetic leadership, and commitment to change and to risk.

4.   Explore various models for continuing one's ministry in a new way.
Denominational staff are often the key to this option, which includes such opportunities as yoked ministry with another parish (a pastor and programming ministries are shared), merging two congregations into a new one, and "nesting" one congregation with another of a different racial/ethnic background (the unique ministry of each congregation is still affirmed and celebrated).

5.   "Fold the tent" and bless the continuing ministry.
The church of Jesus Christ has never been dependent upon buildings, even though buildings may hold precious memories for us and may have been the site of many significant milestones. Memories are to be preserved and celebrated but never worshiped. The closure of a church is like a funeral, but even in a funeral we still celebrate life. It is not the end. Death, as we proclaim boldly, does not have the last word. That word is life, and it was spoken at the cross in Jesus Christ for us for all time.

What Is God Calling Us to Do in This Place?

Many congregations have difficulty praying this question in complete trust that God will provide a clear answer. This is why so many congregations seek to seize control of the decision-making process and force conclusions that seem comforting at the time. Others choose not to choose at all. And some congregations will find themselves praying this question for many months, even several years, until doors to new ministry close, leadership positions go unfilled, the community becomes exhausted, offers are made for their property, or invitations are received to merge or yoke with another parish. How God will answer, no one can say, but prayerfully discerning an answer will yield reward in the end.

NOTES

1. Evangelical Lutheran Church in America Department for Research and Evaluation Report, *The Percentage of ELCA Congregations Which Were Declining, Stable, or Increasing in Average Worship Attendance from 1997 to 2000.*

2. The Constitution of the Evangelical Lutheran Church in America, paragraph 9.03.

3. The Book of Order of the Presbyterian Church (U.S.A.), paragraph 3.0300c.

4. From the work of the New Jersey Synod of the Evangelical Lutheran Church in America, as shared by Bishop E. Roy Riley Jr. in a 1999 letter to the writer.

5. Christian Church Foundation and Board of Church Extension of the Christian Church (Disciples of Christ), "Is it time to fold the tent? When the ministry shifts elsewhere; how to deal with the pain and process," undated.

3

Closing Churches in the Light of American Religious History

Gilson A. C. Waldkoenig

T he subject of church closings is charged with a great deal of anxiety for North American people. The anxiety stems from more than the sense of loss that arises when one loses a community and place held dear. There is a wider social anxiety that is rooted in long cultural experience. Christian experience in North America, from the mid-16th century until today, has imprinted and reinforced a survival mentality among Christians. The survival mentality was rooted in four distinct types of historical experience. The types help to explain the extensive anxiety that wells up around church closings but also can open our vision to possibilities beyond survival and ways to make the adjustment to change. After a look at the four types, we will use them to interpret the trends of church closure in North America to see what the possibilities we might find for moving beyond the collective and historically grounded anxiety by caring appropriately for communities formed by particular histories.

Competition I

In 1564 at the mouth of the St. Johns River, in what is today called Florida, 450 French Protestants established a colony called Fort Caroline. A bell rang out daily to call the pious settlers to worship. Known for their neighborly behavior, nearby Native Americans called the French the "good white tribe" in distinction from the Spanish "bad white tribe." The successful colony was Captain Jean Ribault's second attempt to create a Protestant refuge in America. The first attempt on a South Carolina island failed in 1562.

The settlers at Fort Caroline were honorable, but some other Frenchmen loose in the New World were known to the Spaniards as "Lutheran pirates." Like criminal marauders of other nations, they raided ships and committed murder. In Cuba, the French pirates burned Catholic churches and slaughtered priests as they plundered for gold. Seeking revenge, the Spanish sent 10 ships and 2,700 armed men to establish Saint Augustine, which became the oldest permanent settlement in North America. Their first action was a four-day trip to massacre the settlers at Fort Caroline, in lieu of catching the French pirates. The Spanish captain later boasted to the king about systematic executions and his message to the victims: "I do this not as to Frenchmen but as to Lutherans." His cause was sacred, the conqueror claimed. A few years later, other Frenchmen went looking for Spanish blood in Florida and had their revenge in turn.[1]

The bloodshed in this exchange was tiny compared to the long and terrible religious wars of Europe. It did, however, represent the potential for religiously motivated violence in the American hemisphere. In American history, systematic violence went on against Native Americans, the African captives brought into slavery in America, and some other groups. Other incidences of tensions went on between groups of differing religious traditions, becoming most terribly explicit in anti-Catholic and anti-Semitic incidents. Hence, the early bloodshed on the shores of Florida is a model of both the old-world religious violence and the new-world tensions and violence.

The first church closing in America was the bloody massacre at Fort Caroline, born out of a geopolitical struggle between powers that understood little about the actual religious life of the victims. The national powers vying to build empires treated the little congregation of Protestant believers in whatever way happened to be useful to their wider political and economic causes. The first model of church closing in American memory and experience, then, is one that is brutally imposed by exploitative powers. Closing a church, according to this first experience, is akin to the genocide of the native populations and the enslavement of Africans. It is like the unfair treatment of religious minorities and ethnic groups in American history.

Religious traditions rooted in the established churches, and the would-be establishments, of the warring European nations have had a particularly difficult time adapting to the American environment and modern life. Roman Catholics, Lutherans, Reformed, Anglicans, Congregationalists, and even

Presbyterians were not originally suited to an environment in which they themselves were not to be the established church. Coexistence as "denominations" was only slowly and begrudgingly accepted by these groups. In this model, too, there is no difference between ecumenical and inter-faith relationships: phenomenologically speaking, both are simply competition from which only one "winner" or "survivor" could arise. In this model, establishments, like kingdoms, must be total.

We will have something more to say about denominationalism in one of the other types, below. For now, we note that a certain sluggishness toward religious pluralism is a part of the hangover from the fierce and violent competition of the kingdoms to which certain traditions originally belonged. In turn, if my church is—deep down—the only one that is really supposed to exist, closure is something like getting conquered, based on a zero-sum game in which only one or another religious tradition can occupy any given space. If my church closes, ultimately we have "lost." We have been exploited, conquered, annihilated. There is a deep collective anxiety about church closings that is rooted in the long experience of religious wars and violence.

Frontier I

Just as the French Protestants failed in a South Carolina settlement before Florida, so too the English tried and failed to get their Virginia foothold in 1586 to 1587. The next attempt began immediately in the famous Roanoke colony. The commander of the project left his daughter and granddaughter at the colony. War at sea with Spain delayed supply until 1590, when the whole colony was mysteriously missing. The threat of utter physical failure on the frontier—from the colonial coasts to the inland spaces—leaves an indelible imprint upon the collective American psyche and surely must be jogged at some level every time a church or other institution closes.

Along with a famous New England declaration to build a "city set upon a hill" came a fear of a "howling wilderness" upon which people could die in squalor, become morally corrupt, and revert to an uncivilized state. There was a deep fear of the frontier, reinforced by countless deaths, deprivations, and physical threats. A similar experience repeated itself in many an Appalachian hollow, Midwestern plain, and Western riverbed.

When Virginia was finally stabilized as a colony, plantation settlements presided over by economic entrepreneurs spread out along the tidewater rivers. Although missionary societies extended the ministry of the church by horseback, churches were established largely following the entrepreneurial system. When the entrepreneurs became established, the church could be established as an institution.

The plantation barons in effect succeeded the rulers who were the protectors of the established churches in Europe. The institutional church went from the protective hands of the Holy Roman Emperors to the princes of the kingdoms and nation-states to the coattails of the economic entrepreneurs of North America. A notable exception to that pattern appeared in the communal model, noted below. But in both cases, the institutional church could not survive on the frontier until it had a colonial base of one sort or another, and it had to live by the pattern thus established.[2]

In ensuing frontier expansion across the interior of the continent, the institutional development of the church mirrored the economic development. In prosperous regions, the churches were institutionally established and flourished. In regions where basic survival was difficult, the church took on adaptive forms. Hence, the urban church life of St. Louis, Chicago, and Minneapolis became modernized little by little, while the strenuous and economically marginal Appalachian region retained a pioneer feel.

Largely in adaptation to the frontier, a radical free-choice style of Protestantism developed. The tent revivals did well in the face of weak and absent congregational life. Individual choice and conversion did not depend on the presence of an established community. Meanwhile, small-group systems of organization, such as the American Sunday school movement, proved more effective on the frontier than the older communal forms of congregational life.

Often romanticized and even theologized as Manifest Destiny, the frontier experience was in reality brutal, as historian William H. MacNeill has noted in his worldwide comparisons of colonialism.[3] Perhaps in overcompensation for the challenge of survival on the frontier, there developed a phenomenon called "boosterism." Fueled by speculators who stood to profit from advancing settlers, optimistic promotion of countless towns across the frontier was common even in far-flung reaches. The optimism proved to have tragic consequences in areas where settlement was either impossible or relatively short-lived. But the boosterism had more in common with the mythology of the frontier than the actual frontier context.

In a speech at the 1893 World's Fair, Frederick Jackson Turner delivered his famous thesis on the frontier.[4] It was the frontier that has spurred democracy, he argued, because it fostered the choice and individualism that we previously noted. Unlike MacNeill, Turner assumed that the frontier was a healthy environment, filled with yeoman farmer citizens akin to Thomas Jefferson's ideal. Turner and many with him worried that the frontier was used up and that urbanization was the problematic future of America. Urbanization did proceed, but at the close of the 20th century the city cores also were depleted. The frontier had a new sheen when glimpsed from a suburban window, on one hand, but had reasserted itself as countless rural churches and towns had closed after economic change and population loss.

The second type of church closure from American historical experience is based on the basic physical difficulty of surviving on the frontier. If my church closes, then, it is because we have died of the deprivations that befell countless others before us. Failing at the great task that boosterism enthusiastically articulated, we did not build the church of our dreams. When we close a church, it is as if we go back to the wilderness, reverting to moral degradation and becoming uncivilized. Moreover, there are theological implications that have troubled all Christians on the frontier. When closing, the choice-oriented ask if they made the wrong choices, others must doubt their election, and the churchly types wonder if the choices were illegitimate in the first place. For all, a deep collective anxiety about church closings is rooted in the long experience of the grim realities of survival on the frontier.

Frontier II

Apart from the individualism on the frontier, and in contrast to the independent entrepreneurial pattern of colonial Virginia and elsewhere, there was another pattern of settlement on the frontier. From the Puritan towns of New England to the ethnically homogeneous settlements of the Midwest, often the church was established in congregational form not as a by-product of a wave of individualized choices, and not as an aftereffect of entrepreneurial control of an area, but simply as a community church.

Historian Mark Noll stresses the difference between Puritan New England and colonial Virginia. The former settled for religious and communal reasons, and so towns grew up around churches. In Virginia, the independent entrepreneurs stretched their plantations out of reach of one another, and then the churches were fit in afterwards. Hearkening to the mythical status of the Puritan experience in American life, we ascribe an ideal of religious purity to the independent community church.[5]

Meanwhile, many ethnic communities of the Midwest settled in a communal pattern with the church as the psychic if not physical center. Even in the vast openness of a Minnesota prairie, where even a neighbor's barn is not in view, let alone the church, the church was indeed the communal center of life. The rugged individualism of the German, Norwegian, and Swedish farmers was always tempered by the ethnic communalism. A study by sociologist Sonya Salamon showed how the pattern of commitment to community and place passed from generation to generation among people of German descent, while a more entrepreneurial and less communal style prevailed among those of English descent.[6]

The eventual decline of the highly committed ethnic communities was different from the mere economic decline of the frontier noted above. The ethnic communities of the Midwest declined not so much through economic failure (although this has become the major factor in recent decades with the more recent farm crises). They first declined through economic success, acculturation, the education of succeeding generations, and the ensuing choices of younger generations to move to the cities and suburbs. Although this ethnic type is often not fully distinguishable from the frontier type per se, the sense at a church closing in an ethnic community is different from that of a nonethnic church.

Closing a church that was the center of an ethnic community is acknowledgment of a bittersweet process—the acculturation and dissolution of a once highly cohesive family or tribal unit. Hence, added to the basic loss that is similar to the frontier type described above is the new sense that "now we're just like everybody else." The identity shared with patriarchs and matriarchs, which in many cases extended well back into European roots, is not as strong among the generations going forward in time.

The third type of church closure from American historical experience is based on the inevitable acculturation of once-homogeneous ethnic groups. If my church closes, we acknowledge that "we" are no longer the people whom we had been thinking ourselves to be. By closing our church, we give in to the growing sense that our children belong to the world as much as to the church of my grandfathers and grandmothers. For the local, tribal, family model that is encoded by historical experience into a great number of American churches, closure means losing not only our church, but our family and ourselves as well.

Competition II

The free exercise of religion arose as an alternative to the establishment of religion by kingdoms and their colonies. Principled advocates for freedom of religion were of two types: the rationalists, who yearned for freedom *from* dogma, priests, and the authority of religious institutions; and the pietists, who yearned for a purity of conversion and confession *beyond* the "dead letter" of dogma, the routinized forms presented by priests, and the external authority of religious institutions. Thomas Jefferson became the symbol of the former tradition, authoring the Statute for Religious Freedom in Virginia that led to the free-exercise and nonestablishment clauses in the Bill of Rights. The pietist tradition for freedom of religion was symbolized by William Penn, who founded a Quaker colony but welcomed a diversity of believers. Early American Baptists such as Isaac Backus later took up the crusade for religious freedom on theological grounds.

The last church establishments in the United States hung on until the first decades of the 19th century, despite the clear stance in the new Bill of Rights. The traditions that came from European establishments adjusted only sluggishly to the new environment of increasing religious freedom. In contrast, new movements that put individual choice at the center of their theologies and practices grew exponentially. The 19th century belonged to the Methodist and Baptist types of Protestantism. Old Calvinism gave way to modified forms that downplayed election and honored free choice.

It was a free market for religion, and it seemed to be a dream come true for the free-church traditions. The system of religious freedom mediated and mostly mitigated the old violent competition. It seemed to allow the enclaves of ethnic tribes to persist for a time, except when waves of ethnic hatred swelled. Not every tradition received equal treatment, but a certain amount of freedom came to all. At least theoretically, each tradition was allowed to compete for the free choice of individuals to adhere to it. Those traditions that were not choice-oriented in theology or style could concentrate on helping their own to choose their tradition of origin. And they could help others choose their tradition over others.

The free-market system of religious choice was well adapted to the frontier experience. It mirrored the capitalist economy and seemed to be democratic in its elevation of the authority of individual choice. At times it passed for the "civil religion" or the actual religion of the Republic. When by the 1960s Roman Catholics and Jews were finally perceived with

Protestants as being the three "Judeo-Christian" faiths, they had gained a place in the mainstream of American society. By the end of the 20th century, interfaith pluralism had become publicly accepted, based upon the same underlying free market of religion.[7]

When a church closes, the free market of religion is the ideology that is understood by Americans as basic and unquestionable. Hence, a church closing means that we, our community, and our faith are disposable. Few people question whether or not the system itself is appropriate or right, either theologically or practically. Each congregation is on its own, ultimately, in competition with all others for its own survival. The free-market system of religious choice is what causes the "de facto congregationalism" that sociologist R. Stephen Warner has noted.[8] The free-market system has a well-known drawback: it fosters a kind of consumerism in religion. Critics have labeled it "pick and choose religion" and talk about people's "church shopping." The fourth type of church closure from American historical experience is based on losing the competition for individual congregational success. If my church closes, it is because we did not get enough other consumers to consume our product. The capitalist analogy is reductionistic but pervasive. A deep collective anxiety about church closings is rooted in the whirl of new options and the quixotic nature of human "adherence."

Aggregate Trends

The overall trend in American religious history has been toward church growth and the establishment of new churches. Thousands of churches, however, have closed along the way. Statistics concerning the growth and decline of religious institutions and numbers of adherents are inconsistent, because religious groups throughout American history have counted themselves in various ways and sometimes not at all. Comparing one denomination to another, and one period to another, is not possible except in broad, general terms. Using broad strokes, however, a few scholars have identified aggregate trends from which we may infer trends of church closings.

A wave of decline hit the colonial establishment churches around the time of the American Revolution and into the early 19th century. Hardest hit at that time was the Episcopal Church, but Congregationalist and Presbyterian denominations also suffered losses amidst schisms. Population began to move from colonial shores across western New York and the old Northwest, and some New England towns saw decline. Each of the older denominations adopted new styles to pursue mission on the frontier and in the new free-market environment. They established many new churches in competition with the newer Methodists and Baptists, but undoubtedly many of their congregations in depleted New England towns closed.

Waves of immigrants fueled the growth of the Roman Catholic and Lutheran churches from the 1830s into the 20th century, eventually making Roman Catholics the largest religious group by far and Lutherans the third largest Protestant group after the Baptists and Methodists. For all other groups, the 19th century was also a time of growth. New movements such as Shakers, Mormons, and others grew with the advancing frontier populations. While growth and church planting were the order of the day, the rhetoric of church leaders focused on the "irreligion" of the population on the frontier and in the teeming cities.

In the late 19th and early 20th centuries, the rhetoric began to shift to include concern for depleted or declining churches. A wave of concern for rural and small town churches arose in the publications of mainline denominations. Sociologists Roger Fincke and Rodney Stark have argued that the "rural church crisis" identified by mainline Protestant leaders was not a true decline of churches and adherents in rural areas and small towns. It was only a decline in certain denominations. Other groups, which the mainline leaders did not respect as equals, were growing in rural places at the same time mainline leaders were noticing decline.[9]

Rural demographic and economic decline was uneven throughout the 20th century, with some areas declining precipitously and others experiencing growth. The Great Depression affected the churches, and some observers identified a parallel religious depression. The aggregate rural population has consistently grown in North America along with the total population, but certain areas have seen dramatic decline, especially in the second half of the 20th century. When white flight hit the nation's cities beginning in the 1950s, urban churches suffered decline, but the church planting went on in the growing suburbs. During the same period, the children of ethnic rural communities in the Midwest flocked to the suburbs and left the farming industry that was becoming technological and consolidated.

In the 1970s, mainline denominations began to notice a downturn in membership, and church closings eventually came along. By this time, some of the free-choice denominations of the 19th century were looking like mainline establishments. Assessing the losses and gains of "market share" in the American religious environment since 1940, Fincke and Stark calculated a 70 percent decline for the Disciples of Christ, a 56 percent decline for the United Church of Christ (Congregationalist and Reformed traditions), a 49 percent for Presbyterians, and a 48 percent for United Methodists. Meanwhile, Assemblies of God grew in market share by 371 percent; the Church of God (Cleveland, Tenn.) by 260 percent; Nazarenes by 42 percent, and Southern Baptists by 32 percent.[10]

The largest survey of American congregations, Hartford Seminary's *Faith Communities Today* (2000), showed that evangelical Protestant groups planted 30 percent of new churches before 1945, equal with moderate Protestants (Methodist, Disciples, and Lutherans). In the period 1945–1965, the rate for evangelicals shot up to over 50 percent, while the moderates flattened to a level comparable to liberal, Catholic, African American, and non-Christian groups (between 10 and 15 percent). Evangelicals kept growing and established 60 percent of the new church starts by the year 2000. Only the non-Christian groups worked their way out of the cellar on church starts, reaching 20 percent by the year 2000, while all other groups sank below 10 percent.[11]

Most groups showed an increasing gap in church size by the end of the 20th century. A few very large churches served a disproportionate number of adherents, while the majority of congregations were very small. In the UMC, just 7 percent of the congregations had average worship attendance over 350 in the last decade of the 20th century, while one-third had fewer than 35. ECUSA had 4 percent over 350, and 35 percent with fewer than 50. PCUSA had 7 percent over 300 and one-fourth between 20 and 50 on a Sunday. ELCA had 10 percent of their congregations with over 300 and one-fourth between 20 and 60. Even Southern Baptists had just 6 percent over 350 and one-fourth fewer than 55, and Assemblies of God had 7.5 percent over 300 and one-third between 20 and 50.[12]

Overall, researchers' findings are consistent. The Hartford study found that over 50 percent of North American congregations had fewer than 100 regularly participating adults in worship each week.[13] Lyle Schaller calculated that over half of Protestant churches in America had fewer than 100 in worship on an average Sunday, and two-thirds had fewer than 75. The level of congregations worshiping with fewer than 100 reaches 72 percent among the UMC, 66 percent among the SBC, 65 percent among both the Disciples and the AG, and 50 percent of the ELCA, according to Schaller's counts.[14] Religion writer David Yount cites fewer than 75 members for half of the nation's churches. Yount asserts that "these churches are dying at the rate of 50 every week in America."[15]

Given the aggregate data, the death rate must be hitting the mainline Protestant denominations the hardest. The Evangelical Lutheran Church in America is an example that would stand for the others, because it is the largest denomination from the third largest family in American Protestantism. It is also solidly "middle" in socioeconomic profile. Of its approximately 11,000 congregations, the ELCA closed 1,153 during the last dozen or so years of the 20th century. Another 252 consolidated or merged, and 168 withdrew from the denomination. Among the latter category would be many congregations that disaffiliated when they were on the brink of closure according to synodical or denominational standards. Hence, the ELCA lost about 1,500 congregations in the closing years of the 20th century. Much closer in size to other denominations than the Methodists and Baptists who outnumber it, the ELCA losses are slightly more dramatic than some denominations and somewhat less so than others.

Interpreting Church Closure
through Historical Experience

Without reflecting upon all four types described above, chances are most people will unwittingly think about closing in terms of the fourth type. As if all religious matters could be reduced to personal choice, we tend to think the real issue behind every church closure is the reality of free competition. Acculturated to believe that free competition is fair and good, the plight of a closing church is reduced to the personal stress of those individuals who tenaciously hold on to a church that others do not care to choose. Little thought is given to the wider social implications of church closure. The glib assumption would be that some other church will grow up somewhere else where people want it.

Much more is happening than a mere shift in religious consumerism, however. The church closures are disproportionately distributed among the older denominations— not only the old religious establishments that waged war in the Competition I type of historical experience, but also the historically free-choice traditions that used to be successful in the Frontier I type of historical experience. Those who suffer the legacy of Frontier II experience will lose a sense of family and self with every church closure. Merely encouraging former members to make a new choice will fall flat or be offensive. Offers of new and better possibilities will not be automatically appealing to those whose traditions were formed by Competition I, Frontier I, or Frontier II heritages.

Formulating a new mission and fresh motivation is surely not precluded by the historical formation of the mainline Protestant traditions. But the source and shape of this formulation is not self-evident. Worse, encouraging new mission and motivation might be received as succumbing to the Competition II environment, where mainline traditions are neither native nor fully adapted yet. Whatever the possibilities for the future may be, people will not understand the ultimately life-giving role of church closures without getting free of the dominant free-market mindset born of the Competition II heritage as well as the formative influences of other historical experience.

All four historical experiences have engrained a survival mentality among American religious people. Understanding the four types that inform congregations in various ways will help us move from survival mentality to new vision, avoid foisting upon a congregation a future that is radically out of step with the resources and capabilities that it brings to the task, and make good decisions about when to close. Knowing which historical movements most affect one's congregation will help congregational leaders to assess what needs and fears are most basic.

Similarly, the primary theological issues that must be addressed will be informed by the congregation's historical roots. If basic survival is threatened by a church closing (Frontier I), then the problem of why God lets bad things happen to good people would be a paramount theological issue in that situation (even if few can articulate it). But to a group formed in a Frontier II environment, it is not God's faithfulness but our own and that of our children that is the theological issue. To reassure people of God's justice (a Frontier I response) at a congregational closing in a Frontier II experience would be to unduly heighten the guilt of the people. Similarly, to talk much of new choices and possibilities, á la Competition II, before dealing with Frontier II issues, would be to increase a sense that this generation and its children have abandoned the ways of God. Hence, each congregation will need different kinds of pastoral care and decision-making processes regarding closure, according to the basic type of historical experience that informs it.

NOTES

1. Martin E. Marty, *Pilgrims in Their Own Land: 500 Years of Religion in America* (New York: Penguin, 1984), 41–44.

2. Mark Noll, *A History of Christianity in the United States and Canada* (Grand Rapids, Mich.: Wm. B. Eerdmans, 1992), 51–53.

3. William H. McNeill, *The Global Condition: Conquerors, Catastrophes and Community* (Princeton, N.J.: Princeton University Press, 1992), 5–31.

4. Frederick Jackson Turner, *The Frontier in American History* (Mineola, N.Y.: Dover, 1996), chapter 1.

5. Noll, *A History*, 51–53.

6. Sonya Salamon, *Prairie Patrimony: Family, Farming and Community in the Midwest* (Chapel Hill, N.C.: University of North Carolina Press, 1992). Salamon argues that this difference is ethnic. Germans did choose better land, with an eye to long-term residence for future generations.

7. The writings on the development of the free market religious environment are numerous, but the newcomer to this topic may be the classic by Sidney Mead, *The Lively Experiment: The Shaping of Christianity in America* (New York: Harper & Row, 1963). See also Martin E. Marty, *Righteous Empire: The Protestant Experience in the United States* (Doubleday, 1970).

8. R. Stephen Warner, "The Place of the Congregation in the Contemporary American Religious Configuration" in *American Congregations*, Vol. 2, edited by J. Wind and J. Lewis (Chicago: University of Chicago Press, 1994), chapter 2.

9. Roger Finke and Rodney Stark, *The Churching of America: Winners and Losers in Our Religious Economy*, 1776–1990 (New Brunswick, N.J.: Rutgers University Press, 1992), 202–36.

10. Finke and Stark, *The Churching of America*, 248.

11. Carl S. Dudley and David A. Roozen, *Faith Communities Today: A Report on Religion in the United States Today* (Hartford, Conn.: Hartford Seminary, 2001), 10.

12. Lyle Schaller, "What Is Your Favorite Number?" *Net Results* (May 1997), 13–14.

13. Dudley and Roozen, *Faith Communities*, 8.

14. Schaller, "What Is Your Favorite Number?" 13–14.

15. David Yount, "Amazing Grace: Religious Dropouts," Scripps Howard News Service, 2001.

4

The Members' Experience

Tanya Stormo Rasmussen

Little has been written about the increasing phenomenon of churches being faced with the need to acknowledge their death or ending—an emotionally and spiritually challenging task. I know that I wished desperately for some resources—anything that might have helped me to know how best to minister to the congregation I served as it undertook the difficult emotional journey toward death and emerged as a new creation on the other side. In this chapter I will offer some personal reflections about the members' emotional journey. Clearly, as a pastor, I cannot speak personally as one who was a member—and I do believe that my experience as a pastor was in significant ways very different from that of the members. As such, there will probably be gaps in my observations, and not every member of a congregation would necessarily agree with all my descriptions. But the people I helped to shepherd through a graceful and healthy (but not always easy) journey toward death and new life shared a great deal with me regarding their emotions and spiritual experiences along the way, and I hope that the reflections they shared and the experiences we held in common might be helpful to another congregation undertaking this journey.

Although I was not a member of the congregation I served, in order to connect with the emotional journey of members, I tried mentally to do everything in my power to "become" one of those members. I tried to listen carefully, deeply, and constantly to the stories of each member. And I tried to help members connect their personal and corporate stories with the stories that guided and shaped that congregation's identity. Every congregation needs to be reminded of the many ways its story participates in the lively, living stories of Scripture and its religious tradition. If congregations can recognize the small and grand ways that they have participated in and still are part of the larger cycle of God's created and creative order, they will be well on their way to understanding that in God's economy not one bit of life is wasted. Even the tiny kernel of wheat that falls to the ground and dies gives rise to a field of grain that can feed a multitude (John 12:24).

Too often, congregations become like the pious rich man who approached Jesus by night. Remember what happened? Faithful and devout in so many ways, he walked sadly away from Jesus when he realized that his possessions and identity here on earth were more attractive to him than the promise of eternal life. So, too, many congregations sadly turn away from the promise of new life for themselves and others. Often they are unable to release themselves from the fierce grip that "building bondage"— enslavement to memories, identities, icons, and other treasures associated with a specific building and its history—has on both psyche and soul. Even those of us who believe in the promise of resurrection do not easily relinquish our hold on what is known and controllable, so that we might risk losing everything in order to enjoy life eternal.

The congregation I served had been in a state of decline for more than 30 years. By most accounts, the decline began at the same time a campaign was undertaken to build a new sanctuary. Some members recall the hope and excitement of that time. Others recall only the weekly sermons demanding that they give more in order to defray the debt they had incurred to build their beautiful new sanctuary. The congregation was challenged by a long string of short-term pastorates (most were between two and five years) after its building expansion, especially following the decision to move to half-time status. Each new pastor brought hope and energy for renewal, but within a short time, both pastor and parish were disappointed by the insurmountable obstacles to growth. I was the last of a series of pastors who, with the congregation, had worked very hard to revitalize the parish's ministry. But it became clear to a few lay leaders, our district superintendent, and me after three years together that the time had come for the congregation to release itself (or be released) from its building bondage and to move into the greater, more life-giving future God had in store for us.

I was blessed and greatly advantaged, I think, to have a congregational consultant to help navigate what was for all of us uncharted territory. Her role was to serve as an objective "deep listener" and interpreter for all of us: to help pastor, congregation, and conference authorities hear each other and feel heard by the other. She could help all of us to hear what God was saying to us through our own words and voices.

When I discovered the lack of resources for a congregation faced with ending, I turned to those who have worked with terminally ill individuals and extended their ideas to the congregation itself. Elizabeth Kübler-Ross's work, in her landmark book *The Stages of Dying*,[1] was helpful in a very practical sense. It helped me identify and name some of the social behaviors manifested by members of the congregation as we undertook our journey together. I will talk about the five stages she names (denial, anger, bargaining, depression, and acceptance) later in the chapter. Another resource, Kathleen Dowling Singh's observations in *The Grace in Dying*,[2] helped me to reflect on the powerful identity issues involved in a journey toward death. Just as terminal patients are confronted with questions about who they have been and what their lives have meant, so members of a congregation faced with its imminent end are compelled at many levels to deal with questions about identity and meaning.

Death and Identity

For those who have been life-long, faithful members of a congregation, contemplating its ending compels the individuals to contemplate their own death. In a real sense, many members will feel that the "death" of the church is part of their own death. As such, it is important to hear the personal subtext beneath their questions and comments. One of the most common private fears I heard expressed as I sat with members was, "Who will bury me?" The subtext, I am certain, was this: "Will I ever again be known and feel that I have a community who will remember me in death as they have in life?" The fear, primarily felt by the congregation's eldest members, is that if they go to another church, they will not have time to acquaint themselves with that new community in a way that feels as much like "family" as the present church, the source of so much goodness for them.

Several individuals in our congregation had literally grown up in the church—if not from infancy, then from marriage, through childbirth and marriage of their own children, and for some, through the death and burial of a spouse or children. One such member shared poignantly with me, "I don't know who I am apart from this church." As I continued to talk with her, the subtext emerged: "I have dedicated 60 years of my life to serving in this congregation. Bake sales, church suppers, committee and board meetings, teaching Sunday school, worship every Sunday. My children were all baptized here. My husband was buried from this church. Everything that's sacred to me has a place in this church." Members who make such comments might not know who they are apart from the dying church. It is all they have ever known, and they might not be able to imagine getting into a new routine, going to a new sanctuary every week, or meeting new people. Becoming part of a new church seems like it will take too much energy—and they thought they were supposed to be done with all of that. Anxiety, alienation, and despair are prominent among the emotions they experience.

People commented often about how much they appreciated the sense of security and weekly rhythms of the church they had known for so long. They also valued the sense that the congregation truly was family for most of the members; a good number of folks had no family yet living, or their family lived a great distance away. The fear of alienation from the only remaining "family" these individuals had could be dramatic. Although they all lived within several blocks of each other, many of the older members only got out of their homes on Sunday mornings, which made their time together even more precious. "I can't go to another church; all of my friends are here," one member admitted. And another, "If this church closes, we'll probably all go in different directions, and that will be terrible. What's left of my family lives too far away to see regularly. These folks are my family. They're the ones who take care of me, and I take care of them. That's what family is all about."

Then there were those to whom the building and its various rooms and niches were a source of sacred connection to dearly beloved, departed ones. To them, to lose their church meant loss of regular contact with sacred memories and sacred spaces. One middle-aged woman helped me to understand this when she said, "My grandparents were founding members of this church. My mother was one of the first children baptized here. All of them were buried from this sanctuary." What I heard clearly as her subtext was this: "Every time I come into this sanctuary, I connect in a special way with the spirit of my mother and grandparents. If they close the doors and tell us to go somewhere else, I will be losing that place of sacred connection for myself."

The despair that some members may experience may manifest itself in a number of ways. Certainly, the middle-aged woman who wrote a letter to a local ecumenical authority (who had no prior direct relationship with our congregation), pleading with her to take some sort of public action against her pastor and conference leadership, was desperate. Likewise, the elderly woman who challenged the district superintendent to "make a name for himself" by doing something to "save" the church was desperate. When I approached these members to talk about their actions, I learned that both of them had spent a great deal of time thinking about what had gone wrong and who could have stopped it, and feeling despair that no one seemed to know how to solve the problems. They, too, were filled with anxiety about the possible dramatic change in relationships among the church family that had cared for them across the years—one from childhood, the other through the sickness and death of her husband. I think the despair of members was rooted in an inability to locate the answer that would make everything okay again. Most of them had been around long enough to remember the glory days of the church, and the despair had been mounting for years as they had faithfully carried out their various ministries in the congregation, only to find that decline had nonetheless persistently beset them.

Although most members of the church were confident that God had not abandoned us, there were a couple who wondered aloud where God was in all of this. They still cried out to God but in the spirit of the psalmist lamented the silence of the Lord. In fact, most members, when asked how they felt about God and how they thought God felt about them, offered relatively rote answers: "Of course, I know God is with us. Of course, I know that God loves us. God alone can see us through this." But some were honest and open about their private musings. Some of the questions I heard expressed, not necessarily explicitly, were these: In a culture obsessed with success—especially as measured by numbers and dollars—what does our church's inability to pay the bills and attract new people say about us as individuals? Are we a failure or disappointment to God? Has God given up on us? Is God "with" the "successful" churches in a way that God is not "with" us? Do the bigger, more active churches glorify God more faithfully than we do? Am I a personal failure in faith if I am associated with a church that cannot seem to stay alive on its own? What does it say about God's faithfulness to us—if we die (as a congregation), even after trying to live, does it mean God has abandoned or stopped loving us?

Members of a congregation journeying toward its end need to be aware that God is among them. They need to be reassured constantly of their sacred worth, their utter loveliness in God's eyes. They also need to be reminded of the promise and hope of resurrection and encouraged to look forward with determined faith toward the brighter, more glorious future God is already preparing for them. Throughout this sacred journey, the congregation and pastor will be reminded frequently of their clumsy humanity and rough-hewn nature by the conscious and unconscious actions of everyone involved.

Stages of Death

It is striking that although most members of a congregation in critical condition are not themselves on the brink of physical death, the five emotional states identified by Elisabeth Kübler-Ross in dying patients (denial, anger, bargaining, depression, and acceptance)—along with their accompanying behaviors—have clear parallels in dying congregations.

Denial

For almost every congregation facing death, denial is a subtle yet extremely powerful force that has been at work for many years. For some congregations, the most difficult task will be to acknowledge the hold that denial has exerted and continues to exercise over them. Denial may enable many folks to regroup and get on with life after a dramatic or identity-threatening experience, but denial ceases to be useful when it is no longer temporary. The temptation in denial is to re-create history in such a way that the offensive reality no longer exists and to erect emotional barriers and practice techniques for holding at bay the full emotional impact of one's loss or sense of disempowerment. Most of the time, denial is not even a conscious behavior, but its manifestations can be obvious to the world around, and it can be the ultimate undoing of an individual or a congregation.

A congregation that is beginning to consider closing is breaking through its denial. Nonetheless, some members will insist, "Things really aren't as bad as people are making them out to be. After all, we still have a good number coming to church each Sunday—certainly more than the Baptist church across town! Hey, we're paying our apportionments, and most of our bills are up-to-date. And, besides that, doesn't the Bible say that 'Wherever two or three are gathered, there Christ is in the midst of them'? (Matt. 18:20). I'd say we have plenty more than three here. . . ."

When challenged with the question of whether faithful ministry required more than a family chapel ministry (Sunday worship and visiting the sick and homebound), members of the congregation I served indignantly responded, "Listen, we reach out to people in different ways than most churches. When I think about all of the lives that each member of this church touches, just by spreading a little cheer or happiness, then I think that God's work is being done through the people of this church. It's just not the kind of ministry that you can quantify or record on paper." I was sympathetic to their resistance to quantifying and recording statistics regarding church growth and revenue. Concern with the bottom line is not necessarily compatible with the church's call not to imitate the world's way of doing things. Nonetheless, members resisted being held accountable to the traditional mission of the church, to reach out to bring others to a saving knowledge of God's love and grace.

Anger

One of the primary emotions that is held at bay by the coping mechanism of denial is anger. Because many people of faith believe that the expression of anger is sinful or destructive, they choose to repress the emotion—to stuff it down deep within their souls, rather than praying for constructive ways of expressing it. For congregations moving through the season of death, anger may be felt—and eventually expressed—toward many different entities. There may be real anger about the uncontrollable forces of change that have affected their congregation's historical way of being in their community.

People may express frustration and anger about prior past events, such as clergy, lay, or institutional breaches of trust—whether sexual, financial, or emotional. There were several people in the congregation I served who felt a great deal of anger toward conference authorities, whom they perceived as betraying them and caring only about the "flagship" churches. A small minority of members thought that the bishop and district superintendents were happy to go to the churches that contributed more generously to the financial workings of the conference in order to keep the "wheels greased." The members believed that the smaller, less glamorous churches were not worth judicatory leaders' precious time . . . until there was a crisis, at which time they came in to "lay down the law."

People might also focus anger on a member or members who have traditionally held a great deal of power within the congregation—not the least of which may be the pastor herself—for decisions that were made or persuasively presented ideas that proved to be ineffective. It turned out that many members of the congregation I served, for example, had carried around repressed anger for decades over the building project they believed at the time was untenable but that they nonetheless felt pressured to undertake by a well-intended pastor, lay leadership council, and conference authorities.

Perhaps most difficult for many members to admit will be the anger that a number of them feel toward God. In the minds of many, there is a real sense in which God has "allowed" their decline to happen, and the defiant question becomes, "But why?"

Members of a congregation faced with closure need permission and safe space in which to feel and express their anger. One useful exercise our congregational consultant led involved naming sources of irritation or anger regarding the church, with the accompanying exhortation that, upon naming it, we release the anger and avail ourselves of God's healing in order to move forward. The exercise was deliberately held in the sanctuary, with the participating members sitting in the choir loft, flanking the altar. What an incredible moment of catharsis and enlightenment we experienced as we named the legion of demons that had preyed upon the souls of the people for years—and released them! Naturally, it is critical before undertaking such an exercise to emphasize the need for respectful expression and compassionate listening. But when planned carefully and undertaken prayerfully, this kind of rite can be incredibly liberating and healing.

Bargaining

When it becomes clear that a congregation is faced with closing its doors, it is not unusual for bargaining to begin. Just as the disempowered devil tried to strike a deal with Jesus during his time of temptation in the desert (Matt. 4:9), so will desperate members try to coerce the "powers that be" to give them a chance. It was not uncommon to hear members argue that the conference authorities, which had a consistent role in our discontinuance process, ought to "leave us alone—after all, we're paying our apportionments, and all of the bills are getting paid." The subtle, but mistaken, understanding was that the conference and local United Methodist churches have an implicit agreement: the local church pays the bills and stays out of trouble, and the conference authorities leave them alone. When asked to describe how this local church had been faithful in ways other than just toeing the line, some members contended it was the conference (the institution) that had not lived up to its end of the "deal." It was the contention of some that, if they paid the "bills" (apportionments), then the money they sent to the conference ought to result in some concrete suggestions and effective solutions to counteract their history of decline.

Others simply could not forgive the conference for allowing or encouraging their building project to take place 30-plus years ago in a neighborhood that was predominantly Catholic—and then expecting them to be able to "keep up" with other churches of similar size without bailing them out.

One of the most poignant and painful moments of our congregation's journey together through the difficult meetings of discernment and truth-telling about our future occurred when our district superintendent was present. A 94-year-old woman I mentioned earlier, no longer able to contain her anger and frustration with the lack of control she felt over losing what had been a lifetime church home for her, trembled with emotion as she shook her fist at the authority figure and challenged him, "Why don't you *do* something? Why don't you make a name for yourself—*save* this congregation, and make a real name for yourself? You have the power, so why don't you do *something*?" The feeling of helplessness was common, as was the suspicion that somebody—or some*bodies*—in positions of authority or oversight actually possessed a "magic solution" that would solve all of the congregation's problems, but they were withholding the information. As such, there was a corresponding sense in which some members thought that they needed to figure out and implement this magic solution—to strike the right bargain—in order to be "allowed" to continue.

Depression

Many members did not bargain or even realize they were angry, but most people felt an undeniable sense of depression. We feel profound sadness when losing a loved one, and several members said they felt as if a family member had received a death sentence or a diagnosis of terminal illness. The disempowerment, the loss of a sense of control and identity, and the forthcoming loss of connection with sacred spaces and the sacred memories the impending closing evoked all were enough to burden and sometimes overwhelm members with feelings of depression. Some members coped by avoiding church; some wept openly during worship services. Some were more prone to sickness and fatigue than they had before. Many spoke openly of their deep sadness every Sunday as they entered an increasingly empty sanctuary and wondered, "Where is everybody?" The younger families admitted feelings of guilt and remorse: they wanted to support the church and the families who had helped to build it, but they also wanted to provide a positive experience for their children, and they just were not experiencing a "positive spirit" about the place anymore.

The congregation itself often resembled a person in the early to middle stages of depression. Increasingly consumed with its own grief and despair, it lacked spiritual or physical strength to reach out in new, life-giving ways to others. We had our lively moments, to be sure, and the congregation accomplished amazing things given the average age and physical ability of most of its members. But consistently, achievable goals went unmet, and participation in new endeavors was minimal—unless the efforts involved serving the congregation already present.

Acceptance

Thankfully, by the time our journey was complete—when the congregation merged with another—many of the members had come to accept that life would be very different but that it would go on. Some of the congregational leaders were at a place of acceptance far before the process was through, and this difference actually created friction and resentment among the body. Because some members had accepted the fact of their need for death in order for resurrection to happen, they wanted the process to move along more quickly than it did. This caused other members, who were still coming to terms with the fullness of their anger or grief, to feel "rushed"—and resentful. Accusations of "abandoning ship" and betraying the rest of the congregation were bandied about, sometimes disguised with humor and occasionally delivered with outright animosity.

I am convinced that one of the most important activities fostering acceptance was our including all interested members in discussion about whether and how ending ought to happen. Some complained of too many meetings, too much talking, but it was through the hours and hours of talking, sometimes revisiting old issues two and three times, that people gradually came to terms with the realities at hand. The congregation was invited to name "Things We Must Not Lose" (the list included: faith and spirituality, friendships, ongoing communication, choir and musical talents, sense of humor and adventure). Members were also invited to suggest ways to create a "healthy ending." By participating in these deliberations, I believe, the members were empowered to help create their own future, rather than allowing circumstances to play upon them and further drain them of spirit, energy, and morale.

Though I am no longer leading this congregation, I have heard from various sources that almost all of the active members of the former congregation are now involved in new church homes—a strong indication of acceptance. The congregation essentially split into two groups. Most former members now participate in the United Methodist congregation created by a merger of our congregation and another United Methodist church. A smaller minority happily participates in a United Methodist congregation in a nearby town. The merged congregation is continuing to work with the consultant who worked with us throughout the discontinuance process to ensure a healthy union between the two merging entities. The few who decided to go to another congregation maintain friendships and frequent connections with those who chose to go to the merged church. In fact, the choirs of both churches are joining forces for joint Christmas and Easter concerts, some of which will be held in the sanctuary of the former congregation!

Toward New Life

There is no question that the closing of a church is difficult for everyone involved, from the most senior member of an ecclesiastical system to the pastor to the youngest self-aware member. But the members arguably experience the most intense emotional and spiritual journey. Congregations on a journey toward ending are greatly blessed if leaders are intent on embracing the process and acknowledging the pain and fear involved but consistently set sights on the promise of resurrection and glorious new life that most certainly awaits each one. Increasing numbers of congregations are undertaking this journey. It is one that can be made with grace and health only if the congregation is grounded in a secure sense of its identity in God, as God's dearly beloved, called to let go of life as they know it, so that more abundant life might be birthed through them.

NOTES

1. Elizabeth Kübler-Ross, *The Stages of Dying* (New York: Collier Books, 1997).

2. Kathleen Dowling Singh, *The Grace in Dying* (San Francisco: HarperSanFrancisco, 1998).

5

The Pastor's Experience

N. Nelson Granade, Jr.

The dam of pent-up emotion broke one Sunday before Emory Baptist Church would cease to exist as a congregation. As if caught up in a torrent of muddy water, I was swept away by fear, anger, and despair. I had helped others navigate grief but was about to lose myself. I had never lost control in the pulpit. I tried to focus on the beautiful offertory our pianist offered but was only reminded that even the music would soon end for our church. Then it happened! No matter how hard I tried to hold it back, wet eyes turned into tears, tears turned into weeping, and weeping turned into sobs beyond control.

I bolted from the sanctuary and ran to the relative safety of my office. The emotions hit me with such strength that I do not even remember my steps. It is said that tears are cleansing, but I felt more like I was drowning. The first thing I remember is the sound of my wife's voice. I did not even realize she was holding me, but her voice broke through the noise of my strife. I clung to her words like a drowning man might cling to anything that would float.

As I began to understand her words, I began to hear my own words as well. She was responding to me as I muttered: "I have a sermon." "The people need me." "I must go back and preach." I said these words over and over, fixated on my task and unaware of my needs. "You don't have to preach." "They can wait." "You have to take care of yourself." Her words were reassuring but difficult to hear in my despair. It was my own soul to which I had not been listening.

In this torrent of emotion, I finally realized an important truth. My church would die, but I did not have to die with it. The flood would not win, nor was it my enemy. The dam was of my own making. The feelings it had held back were too powerful to be controlled for long. They were not meant to be dammed up within anyone's soul. Had I been aware of and expressed more of my own feelings, they would not have burst forth with such intensity.

A Primary Challenge

Guiding others through the joys and pains of life, while trying to negotiate our own feelings, is part of the work of every pastor, but it can be especially difficult for those called to serve dying congregations. We are pulled by the polar temptations of "going down with the ship" or "taking the first life raft." If we allow our spirits to drown, we cannot serve our people and our ministry dies with our spirit. If we jump ship (whether physically or emotionally), we abandon our people and leave our God-given charge. So how do we save others and ourselves, too?

Edwin Friedman, a noted psychologist who brought family systems theory to faith communities, presented a worthwhile goal when he counseled pastors to be a "nonanxious presence." I must admit, however, that when I am dealing with issues of life and death, it is very difficult to be both "present" and "nonanxious." But as a lifeguard must enter the life-threatening waves to save one in danger of drowning, so must pastors enter the turbulent waters of those in pain. We might do well, however, to remember that the first task of a lifeguard is not to allow himself or herself to be drowned by the person he or she is trying to save.

The challenge for pastors of dying churches is to be present in the midst of anxiety and grief without being overcome by anxiety. When performing this balancing act, we pastors often tip to one side or the other. We cannot sustain the needed balance unless we maintain our own center of gravity. As I experienced the death of Emory Baptist Church, I had tilted to the side of trying to take care of others while withdrawing emotionally. When the emotions I feared most finally broke through, something amazing happened: I found healing and unknowingly provided an opportunity for healing.

When I regained my composure and reentered the sanctuary on that horrific and blessed day, I found that a miracle had happened. The people were publicly weeping. They, too, needed to cry and needed their pastor's permission and leadership to do so. My tears had freed their tears, and together we expressed our grief in sacred worship. As one of our guests said of that day, "I felt like I had entered a holy moment between God and God's people." What can happen when people know that you honestly feel their pain is truly amazing.

I went on to preach that day about how a grain of wheat must die and be buried before it can grow into a stalk that produces much more fruit. I reassured our people that in the death of our congregation, the gift of our building to help endow a new school of theology would produce ministry many times over. We spent some time honoring our history. We celebrated accomplishments and tried to let go of our failures. Most importantly, we honestly expressed our grief and said good-bye to an important ministry. By doing so, we freed ourselves to say hello to new opportunities in God's grace.

Sometimes the only way out of a difficult experience is to go through it. You only have the choice of walking away or walking down what seems to be the most painful path possible. A pastor must not only choose to walk this path but has the added responsibility of leading others along it as well. A pastor can only walk such a path healthily by honestly dealing with his or her own emotions, remembering the One who walks with us in the valley of the shadow of death.

Herein lies our strength. We are people of faith, and though we doubt at times, God will carry us to new life. When a congregation dies, leaders, members, and perhaps others experience a significant grief, but who knows how to deal with grief better than the church and its ministers? The question becomes, Can we take our own advice? Can we who minister admit to and deal with our own grief? I contend that by taking care of ourselves, we will be better able to care for others.

Recognizing Our Grief

We know the cycles of grief, but will we recognize them within ourselves and get the help we need to be healthy? I am reminded of a recent tragedy within the community I now serve. A well-respected physician known for his diagnostic wisdom died of a heart attack. He had been experiencing significant shoulder pain but attributed it to a continuing bursitis and did not seek outside medical help. The physician could not heal himself, and we as pastors cannot provide our own pastoral care.

We all know the stages of grief first taught to us by Elizabeth Kübler-Ross, but having the knowledge does not guarantee that we will have the wisdom to recognize and deal with our own feelings. Denial is a strong process, and given that it and isolation are the first stage of grief, we can easily be lulled into believing our own tales. Words such as, "I'm a professional at dealing with feelings," "I need to help others and can deal with this later," or "Everything will be OK tomorrow" are deceptions we can easily believe. In fact, we want to believe them. Few pastors want to admit that the church they serve is dying.

In my own case, the denial was at work early in my relationship with Emory Baptist. A certain amount of denial is probably necessary when a pastor makes the decision to serve any congregation, but it is especially needed if the congregation is in decline. We want to believe things are better than they look, or that we can make them better, or we would never take the call in the first place. We exhibit a purposeful naivete similar to that of a couple falling in love. It is often nurtured by denominational staff who want to help a congregation find a good pastor, and friends who want to see us take on an interesting challenge. As in dating, both the pastor and the congregation try to put their best foot forward. The pastor does not tell all his or her faults, and the congregation does not either.

So I naively accepted the call to a church in steady decline within a transitioning neighborhood. Why shouldn't we be able to turn this church around? Others churches had turned around, and their pastors were hailed as heroes. This church had good leaders, a great facility, and a little money in the bank. Beside all this, churches do not die—or so I thought! God bless those pastors who knowingly choose to help a church close, but I was not one of them. It took a lot of energy, but it seemed easier to maintain the denial than to admit to the approaching death.

Dealing with Isolation

This ongoing denial was soon accompanied by isolation. Few people want to be around death, and I sometimes wonder whether the ones who do are sick or saints. We avoid death because it reminds us of our own mortality. We avoid dying churches because they remind us that congregations are also finite. Like people, congregations have life cycles. The church universal is eternal, but earthbound entities are not. Many congregations live long lives and serve multiple generations, giving the illusion of immortality, but the truth is that no congregation has lived forever. Even the house churches of biblical times have passed from the stage of history.

It is easy to become isolated, because most other churches and other pastors do not want to be reminded of these facts. Widows supposedly wear black as a sign of mourning, but perhaps it is really a sign of warning to those who do not want to encounter grief. Such isolation can follow a pastor long after his or her tenure with the dying congregation. I remember interviewing with several churches that did not want to hear my story of creatively helping a dying congregation through a time of pain. They did, however, want to hear my exploits from when I helped start a new congregation. People like to visit the newborn babies in the hospital, but few want to venture onto the oncology ward.

It is true that others avoid us when we are dealing with death, but it is also true that our isolation can be self-imposed. As we begin to move out of denial, we often move towards depression.[1] When we awake to the fact of approaching death we become angry, and our first response is often to suppress this anger—the very definition of depression. This depression leads us to cut off contact with those who would normally give us support. The depression hangs like a cloud overshadowing us throughout our grief process. We do not want even to be around people, much less minister to them.

Though some people avoided me to avoid my pain, I am grateful to my wife and friends who would not allow me to sink totally into isolation. I marvel at the love of those who both listened to my grief and challenged me to walk through it with faith. Despite the depression that made me want to hide or push people away, I needed people and was fortunate enough to have good friends. I learned that as we move through depression, the healthiest thing we can do is to fight the isolation by purposefully reaching out to others.

Among the best people to whom one might reach out are those with training in counseling or spiritual direction. Though some denominations require supervision for all ministers, many churches that are congregational in their ecclesiology give very little guidance or support to their leaders. I was fortunate to have learned the value of supervision through Clinical Pastoral Education and have made it a point ever since to seek out my own supervisor. I believe no one working with such important matters as the spiritual lives of others should be left without support or supervision.

Another way I found to fight the depression and isolation was to maintain outside interests. During my time at Emory Baptist Church, two of the greatest blessings of my life, my son and daughter, were born. I also entered a doctor of ministry program at Columbia Theological Seminary and wisely chose to do a project on a topic other than the closing of a church. Though it might sound odd, I also found that one of the advantages of serving a dwindling congregation is that I had more free time to pursue other interests.

Whether through continuing education, spending time with family, or pursuing a hobby, every minister needs outside outlets to keep from being engulfed by the ministry. My wife helped me to take my own advice in this matter. In a sermon, I quoted a counselor who asked a physician, "Who are you when you are not being a doctor?" That afternoon my wife turned the question on me and asked, "Who are you when you are not being a pastor?" To be honest, I was not sure, and that was a warning sign to do more outside of the congregation. Whatever the ministry setting, I have found, having a life outside of work is always a good thing. Like any institutions, churches will take whatever you are willing to give them, and ministers who are not intentional about "down time" will not get it.

Reasons for Anger

Most of us who experience a call to ordained ministry have an unwritten contract with God. Some clergy are aware of this contract process, and others have barely given it a thought. Whichever the case, our expectations of ministry directly affect our relationship with our congregation and with God. Consciously or unconsciously, we act as if our part of the contract is to give and give and give in ministry, but we also expect some—often unnamed—blessing in return. Though a few pastors have pursued intentional "hospice" ministries to dying churches, most pastors would consider this type of ministry to be "outside of the contract." The "contract" is to grow (or at least maintain) a church, and we have a hard time imagining there might be blessings in helping a church die.

When we do not receive what we think our contract guarantees but rather discover (or admit) that we are stuck with a dying church, we feel angry. Soon, anger abounds. Parishioners get angry with pastors. Pastors get angry with parishoners. And everyone gets angry at God—though few will admit to it. Churches are not supposed to die. God is supposed to be faithful to God's people. The church is supposed to be a foundation of the community. When we are honest, we can easily see why the temple leaders got angry at Jesus when he announced that "not a stone of the temple would be left upon another." We respond to threats with anger, and few threats are greater than those to what we hold sacred.

For the pastor, the anger involves additional issues. When a church closes, our careers are threatened. No matter how we try to "reframe" it, the closing feels like failure. As we often do when confronting failure, we begin to look for someone to blame. Are we at fault? What did we do wrong? Perhaps it is the church's fault? They were in this mess before we came! Could God be at fault? Can we even think that? Perhaps we need to take a lesson from the psalmist who openly contended with God and trusted God's love enough to frankly plead Israel's case. Did not our Lord honestly express his feelings when he quoted Psalm 22 from the cross: "My God, my God, why have you forsaken me?"

Again, it is hard for us pastors to take our own advice. I have counseled people many times to be honest with God. "God already knows how you feel," I say. "Why don't you go ahead and get it off your chest?" Despite biblical precedent, it is difficult to be honest with God about our anger and frustration. It is easier to adopt a false piety or an unrealistic hope that God will change God's mind. We begin to force the issue and reconstruct our unwritten contract. We want things to be the way we think they are supposed to be, and we are willing to strike any bargain to do it.

Bargaining and Reality

The bargaining phase of grief is an interesting one. My congregation came up with all kinds of plans to attempt to survive, including a reverse mortgage that would have ended up giving the bank a very valuable piece of property. At the same time, I as their pastor was busy with my own bargaining. I hired church growth consultants, visited extensively with denominational workers, invited special speakers, and began a mass-mailing campaign to bring the people in and save the church (never mind that we would not have been able to park their cars if they actually showed up). If I could only find the trick or be more faithful to my call, God would save this church.

Despite my bargaining and that of the members, we finally had to face the fact that Emory Baptist Church would soon cease to be a congregation. The question was not if, but when and how. We were being called to faithfulness but a new kind of faithfulness. As the leader, it fell to me to call the church to this new faithfulness. I will never forget the first time I spoke about the reality of the approaching death of the church we loved. I invited the three key lay leaders of my church to lunch and simply stated the obvious. I talked through all we had tried to do and all that was against our survival. I then simply said, "I don't think our church as we know it can survive. Do you think God might be calling on us to do something creative with the assets God has given us?"

Two of the leaders were almost relieved that someone had spoken openly what we all knew in our hearts: our church was dying. The other was still in the bargaining stage and thought that we should try even harder, but even he could not think of another possibility. I, too, was still willing to bargain and offered two options concerning my leadership. If they wanted to continue to try to survive, I offered to move on and let them hire a part-time pastor. If they wanted to find a creative solution and would take care of me and my family, I would see them through the burial of their church. They decided that going to a part-time pastor would only delay the inevitable and that it was not good stewardship to use God's resources on a church with limited ministry opportunities. Together we made a new covenant to find a creative way to reinvest God's facility and to take care of one another in the process.

With this acceptance, we began the process of leading people to honestly deal with their grief and to look for new sources of hope. Like any leader, a pastor is often emotionally three to six months ahead of his or her people. It took time for us to work together, and we continued in the malaise of the grief process for some time. People were at various stages of denial, depression, anger, and bargaining. It was by no means easy, but little by little members began to find acceptance—and with acceptance—hope.

I can honestly say that I am proud of the people of Emory Baptist Church of Decatur, Georgia, and believe that through its death, the congregation continues to do the greatest ministry of its life. The very week we decided to give our assets to Mercer University, the university decided to accept the gift and commit to a new school of theology in Atlanta. Instead of supporting one small struggling church, the church's gift is funding the education of hundreds of ministers who will spread the gospel throughout the world!

The people of the church turned out okay, too. After I decided that I did not have to die with the church, they decided the same as well and joined in the ministry of a larger, healthier church in our community.

In grateful response, the people of First Baptist Church of Decatur welcomed us graciously, offered our people immediate leadership roles, and called me to be their associate pastor. I will never forget the words of one of the congregation's most faithful women, who after being in the new church for only a month called me aside and said, "We should have done this years ago!" She continued, "It is such a joy to come to church and do ministry instead of having to figure out how we can keep the doors open and lights on for another week."

Our closing felt like failure, but it was success! The reality is that congregations facing their last days have not failed. In fact, a dying church's pastor and leaders are some of the most faithful people you can find. As C. H. "Red" Emmert said to me before I arrived at Emory Baptist (though I thought he was kidding at the time), "I'll be there with you, Pastor. I'll be there till the doors close." With a little leadership and an honest response to grief, he was with me, and so were the many faithful people who faced the death of their beloved church with courage and hope.

Though not every congregation is fortunate enough to have valuable physical assets to pass on, every congregation has a legacy to leave. How a church is able to do that can be influenced in a large part by its pastor. The bad news is that it requires a significant grief process. The good news is that churches are the best folks around at dealing with grief. If we pastors will be honest enough to process our grief, get the help we need, and be faithful to our people, God can still work miracles. The miracles probably will not be the ones you would like or plan, but isn't that just like God!

NOTE

1. Here I disagree with Kübler-Ross's order of the grief process. I think depression often follows denial and isolation instead of anger. Once one begins to get in touch with suppressed anger, he or she can begin to move out of depression.

6

Merger as a New Beginning

Terry E. Foland

Merging two or more congregations[1] can be a way to end the final chapter of those congregations and to begin life in a "reborn" congregation. Merger should not be viewed as a last-ditch effort to keep a struggling congregation open; rather, merger should clearly be the result of members' discerning what God is calling them to be and do and an effort to carry out an exciting new vision of the church.

Merging congregations might seem to be a simple matter of getting together and working out some agreements that will make them one church. But the reality is that many underlying issues, emotions, and practical problems make the process of merging churches a complex and often exasperating enterprise. Merger is not about deciding to work together in a way that allows each congregation to continue as a distinct entity. Nor is it about one congregation being subsumed by another. Merger means closing each congregation in order that a new congregation may be birthed.

Motivations—Good and Bad

What is driving the interest in a possible merger? Is it the result of a decline in membership or participation to the point that the congregation is no longer a viable entity? Have some members become aware of another church in similar circumstances and speculate that if the two join, they will be stronger? Do members have some sense that God may have a new vision for the faithful of this community that includes the possibility of a merger of some congregations?

My own action/reflection research from working with about 70 efforts to merge churches over the past 30 years indicates that when either the only or the primary motivation for merger is survival, most of the time the merger only results in postponing the death of the churches that merged. Survival generally does not provide the motivation for leaders working to save a congregation to think in new ways about how to be the church. As a result, the old patterns and habits of the churches continue, and the culture of the merged congregation contains the seeds for destruction. Putting together two congregations that have both been in serious decline and denial about why they have been in decline will not bring about the necessary changes to foster growth and generate new energy or vitality.

It might seem like a good idea for churches to merge when the pastors are compatible and seem to work well together. Sometimes merged congregations will continue to be served by a pastor from one of the merging congregations. The problem is that if the merger was partially based on the two pastors being able to work together, when one leaves, for whatever reason, the merger may lose some of its guiding direction and energy.

Most often, because a merged congregation can usually afford only one pastor, the congregations think they have to decide which of the pastors should stay and which one should move on after the merger. The best solution, however, is for both pastors to agree to move after a merger is completed and for the new congregation to call a new pastor who will not be a carrier of past traditions or practices that might not be appropriate for the new congregation.

A third poor motivation for merger is the hope that a merged congregation will be more efficient. Sometimes it is the members who observe that both congregations have the expense of a building to maintain and a staff to support, and the two together could operate much more cheaply. Often a denominational executive or other church administrator views the "the big picture" and thinks it makes perfect sense for two congregations that are barely able to stay open to get together and become one. There may be some very good reasons, however, for there to be two congregations of the same denomination within a couple of miles or even a few blocks of each other. One might be oriented toward mission work with the low-income families of the inner city, while the other is attuned to ministry with the middle- and upper-income families of the immediate neighborhood. Should they merge? Probably not, unless they decide together that their understanding of mission could be redefined and include some element of the work each congregation feels called to do. Congregational leaders or other planners might also consider whether the neighborhoods or populations the congregations are serving are as close in their culture and social traditions as they are geographically.

Merger should be approached not primarily as a solution to problems, but on the basis of the gifts and assets each congregation brings to the table. Mergers will work best when the potential partners carefully assess the assets they can bring to a new beginning. Merger might be motivated by desperate situations, but lasting mergers of congregations are the result of a good blend of gifts each partner has to offer for new mission.

Seeking a New Vision and Mission

A successful merger begins, then, with a sense of call about how to use each congregation's gifts. That sense of call must be captured in a new vision—a word or picture that communicates what a congregation can be that it is not now. "We can do these things, or we can be this church together." "God is calling us to be and do something new." Seeking a new vision is largely an exercise in restating the congregation's identity. It is not a simple task, however, for a group of people to change their image of who they are from XYZ Church with a history covering more than six generations of the founding families, to ABC Church requiring new relationships and emotional ties. Only a genuine sense that God is calling a community of faith to do a new thing will be sufficient to sustain the effort needed to move into the new vision. The vision and mission must be owned by the merging congregations as a whole, or they will not result in a new beginning.

Congregations exploring merger often want to get down to the nitty-gritty of practical issues before they have discerned what God is calling them to be and do together. Eventually, the congregations will need to decide: Where will we gather for worship? What about the organ that the Schroeder family gave to this church? If we leave this building, what will we do with the stained-glass windows? Who will the pastor be? Can we still be identified as a Presbyterian church? If we move to their site, how will our people who walk to church get there? What will the name of the church be?

These and many other practical questions will have to be addressed, and satisfactory solutions will need to be found, but they should not be put on the agenda until a new vision and mission for such a new church has been discerned. The questions about how the merged congregations will function can actually thwart a possible merger if there is no clear and inspiring vision and compelling sense of mission. Vision and mission come first. Practical details should be worked out only after the congregations make a commitment to the dream of what might be.

Careful thought must be given to how all of the active members of each congregation can be involved in the discernment process. One model that has worked in many places includes opportunity for members of each congregation to work alone part of the time and for groups of members from both churches to cooperate at other times. The "mixed" groups spend time in prayer, Bible study, and discussion of questions such as, What do we think God is calling us to do and be in this community now and in the future? This model also suggests that the two congregations find specific activities they can do together, such as hosting a joint vacation church school or worshiping and enjoying fellowship.

The third part of this model is to form a joint committee with members from the two churches who listen to the results of the discussions of the two separate churches and write a brief vision and mission statement for the new congregation. The statement is shared in each church for discussion and refinement, and the joint committee receives members' feedback and continues to reshape the statement until there is consensus on the statement.

Polity and History

Whether merging congregations are part of the same denomination or come from different groups, both will have to work within the polity of their denomination if the merger is to receive support of the denominational system. Middle judicatory officials should be involved early in the discussions if merger is a serious possibility. Usually a middle judicatory staff member or volunteer committee member can give advice and counsel regarding mergers. A bishop or other official or governing body might need to approve any merger decision or certain aspects of a merger. Congregations will need to determine whether the church property is owned by the congregation or the middle judicatory (conference, region, presbytery, diocese, synod, or other entity).

Other legal strings attached to the property or financial assets of the church must be explored. Is there a mortgage held by the denomination that helped to finance one of the buildings? Or perhaps a loan for a building improvement has not been paid off? The merging congregations will also need to become familiar with the system for the resignation and calling or hiring of pastors or other church staff.

Mergers across denominational lines are not common, but they can be accomplished in a number of ways. (1) The new congregation decides which of the denominations it will be related to and then ends its relationship to the other denomination. (2) The new congregation becomes a "union church" and chooses to relate in some way to the denominations of both congregations. These two options are the most likely to work long-term, because they are based on a genuine merger that is dependent on full commitment to a new beginning.

Merged congregations might choose other models, however. (3) The new congregation is composed of two legally separate congregations, and each partner continues to relate to its own denomination. The two then make agreements about specific aspects of their work together—using the same building, being served by the same pastor, or sharing some common mission and ministries. (4) The new congregation decides to be independent and is not related to any denomination. (This fourth choice may raise major issues regarding history, identity, and ownership of property.)

History is an issue that must be addressed whether or not the two congregations are of different denominations. What is the story of each congregation? How did it get started, and why was it put in this place? Has it always been at the present location, or has it relocated at some time? What has been its identity and image in the community? Does this church carry some of the culture and identity of the larger community? Does the church have a particular ethnic or racial history? What has been the shape and extent of its ministry and mission? How do the members understand the main purpose for this church continuing its mission and ministry? What would be lost if this congregation closed? All of these questions need to be considered if the congregation is going to move forward as part of a merger into a new chapter of its continuing history.

In addition to understanding its own history, each church must also reflect on the relationship that has existed between the two churches. Has there been a good relationship, or have there been some moments of tension or even open conflict? Have there been joint efforts in mission or ministry in the past? How has that gone? Have there been any attempts to merge these churches before? What happened then? Why did the merger not take place? What factors blocked the movement, and what is different this time? How will those issues or questions be resolved this time?

The relationship between the two congregations has not taken place in a vacuum, and members will need to engage in some candid conversation about how the congregations have been part of the community. Have members of the two congregations taken different positions on a community political issue? Has one congregation been either blessed or cursed by having an influential family from the community among its members? Are community divisions reflected in the make-up of the congregations? These and similar issues can make or break an intended merger and need to be addressed with openness and candor.

Getting It Together

Congregational organization should have only one purpose and that is to carry out the mission of the church. One advantage of a merger is that it can provide the church with an opportunity to free itself from long-held but unnecessary organizational trappings that sap the energy, time, and interests of church members. An effective merger results in organizing the lay leaders of the two congregations in a way that will give fair representation to each of the churches without becoming too large and cumbersome.

One model that has been effective is to create an interim or start-up board that is no larger than the board of the previous congregations but that is made up of an equal number of members from each. The interim or start-up board serves as the governing board for a two-year period, and then a new board with staggered terms of office is started, again with a balance of members from each previous congregation. After six years, the board members are elected without reference to previous church membership.

In one merger of two churches from different denominations, the decision was made to study the practices and norms of both denominations and to create a hybrid organizational structure. The structure included the elements required by each denomination but with a clear understanding that these structures and procedures were designed to enable the new church to meet those denominational standards. This church created what they called a vestry/session and elected members from both denominations. They also chose to relate to both denominations by appointing representatives to attend the various activities of each denomination. They selected people from the "opposite" denomination as representatives to help members begin to understand their new partner's practices.

Another crucial issue is blending various established ministries, traditions, and practices in the new congregation. The key will be to evaluate all activities in light of the vision and mission on which the new congregation is founded. If there is clear evidence that a given ministry helps to move the congregation toward the goals of its mission, then the ministry should be continued. If the ministry does not clearly help to fulfill the mission, it should probably be discontinued. Dropping past ministries will be difficult. Ministries usually benefit someone, and it is hard to stop doing a good thing. In order to accomplish what we believe God is calling us to do, however, we may have to choose to stop doing some good things in order that even greater things can be accomplished.

It may be difficult to continue all of the traditions and practices of both congregations. For example, one congregation may have celebrated communion every Sunday, while the other observed communion one Sunday a month. One congregation might be accustomed to receiving the offering early in the service of worship, while the other has done that following the sermon. But sometimes both congregations' traditions can be maintained. If one congregation has had a five o'clock Christmas Eve service, while the other has had a midnight service of carols and candlelight communion, the merged congregation might decide to hold two services.

At times, congregations have to compromise or negotiate to find the appropriate wedding of the two sets of traditions and practices. At other times, they need to discontinue what each congregation has done and create something new. Most merged churches have welcomed the opportunity to try new things and have found that blending two old ways of doing things ends up producing a better way.

Different heritages may be a bit more difficult to manage because the value to members of each congregation's heritage might be intangible and therefore difficult to articulate. But it will be important to capture members' roots and legacy of faith. The cross that graced the altar in one congregation was a gift from a family that had emigrated from the same country as many other members' ancestors. The cross did not fit the decor of the new sanctuary, but it was put in a prominent place in the building as a reminder of the forebears' faithfulness to God. One congregation owned a beautiful hand-carved board on which the hymns for each week's worship service were listed in Swedish, although most of the members of that congregation could no longer read Swedish. The hymn board was hung in the sanctuary of the new merged congregation, and the person who had posted the hymns continued to do so as a reminder of the faith legacy the members had received from others.

Dealing with the Knotty Details

Many congregations would rather continue toward a certain, slow death than deal with the difficult and intricate issues essential for moving them to new life through a merger. When a congregation has been in decline for several years, even decades, inertia seems to set in, and making decisions that would reverse the trend is very difficult. Six knotty issues, some of which have been discussed above, seem to be at the heart of most congregations in decline, and if these are not resolved, they keep the congregation on a path toward eventual closure.

The first and probably the most difficult issue is the resistance of lay leaders to making any of the real changes necessary for a successful merger. The vision and call to mission will need to be sufficient to compel the lay leaders to move into threatening territory, where they may be asked to share leadership with others from a different church. The current lay leaders will need to have a high commitment to setting a new and exciting vision, or they will sabotage the dream. It is important for the core lay leaders of the congregations considering merger to do some team building and dreaming together, so that the threat of their own loss as leaders can be minimized.

The second issue is reluctance to change staff, some of whom may have been around a long time. By their mere presence, these staff can contribute to the inertia of the situation. The pastor might be only a few years from retirement, and members "don't want to cause difficulty for her in these waning years of ministry." This pastor might be well loved, and no one wants to hurt her, but she does not have the vision, energy, or leadership qualities necessary to help create new life for this church by exploring a merger. So the church waits, and while waiting, continues to decline. Or resistance might focus on a beloved church musician who does not have the interest or ability to lead music that would help attract potential members. The need for staff changes is a major factor when considering merger as a way to new life.

Identity is the third difficult issue. "We have always been known as the 'little country church.' That is who we are. If we merge with the church in town, we will lose that identity." "We have always been Presbyterian.

If we merge with a Disciples of Christ congregation, how will we know who we are?" The vision for moving congregations into a merger must be sufficiently compelling to overcome the powerful forces that seek to maintain an identity.

Where will we worship? Congregations worship in sacred space. Any plan for working toward a merger will need to consider carefully the emotional ties that people have toward the place where they have worshiped God. Some members grew up in this congregation. They were baptized and confirmed here. They were honored here when they graduated from high school and college. They and their spouse spoke their wedding vows here. They were comforted here when they said final good-byes to members of their family who died. This is sacred space. The sacred space can also extend to the education and fellowship space. In many instances, there is a cemetery on the church grounds where family members are buried. If the issue of sacred space is not addressed and satisfactory solutions found, members will not support a merger.

The selection of a name for the merged new church is also a difficult task. The name of a church communicates who these people are collectively. First United Methodist Church implies that this church has been here for a long time and was the first of its denomination's congregations in this area. It also provides a "brand" name: these people are Methodist, not Roman Catholic or Mormon or Baptist. The name might reflect the history of the merged churches or communicate something about the new vision. The very process of selecting a new name can be a channel for putting closure on the past and building commitment for the future. Name is important.

The sixth and final difficult issue is integrating the members of the two churches into one community. This task requires both honoring members' existing relationships, on the one hand, and developing a sense of inclusion and openness to new relationships, on the other. Bringing members together in a merged congregation will demand great sensitivity and tact. People will be threatened if they think they are going to lose the groups in which they found their own grounding in the church. Will we still have the Tuesday quilting group? Will the women's Bible study class continue? Can we combine some groups? Fear of losing intimate connections can block movement toward a new church.

Case Study of a Merger

Two congregations I was invited to work with offer what I think is a particularly inspiring story of a successful merger that was truly based on each congregation's gifts and a compelling vision for ministry together.

St. Paul is a United Church of Christ Congregation with a history going back to 1848 as a congregation of the Evangelical and Reformed denomination. It resisted the 1957 merger of the Congregational Christian Church and the Evangelical and Reformed Churches that created the United Church of Christ. In 1964, the congregation voted to join the UCC and at the same time voted to relocate. The membership at the time of the move was about 350, and the congregation built a facility that would eventually house a congregation of about 600 active members.

The housing developers, however, made a decision to skip over a large territory adjacent to the church and built most of the new houses more than five miles from the church site. The denomination also decided to start a new church near the new housing development, and St. Paul did not grow but began a steady decline. By 2000, there were only about 50 active members and an average worship attendance of 25 to 30. There was essentially no Sunday school, although one teacher was always available in case someone with children showed up (which hardly ever happened). There was no adult Sunday school. A choir of six or seven people sang most Sundays.

The church had parking space for about 100 cars and property for expansion when needed. The church still had a debt of about $800,000 on the building, and needed repairs to the roof and window would cost about $250,000 if done right. The operating budget was about $80,000, of which $65,000 was for utilities and staff, including a part-time interim pastor and paid organist.

Third Presbyterian Church was founded in 1956 on the growing edge of the city, about a mile and a half from St. Paul and on the same major street. The congregation built a two-unit facility, one housing the sanctuary and offices; the other, an education building. The original plans called for a large sanctuary to be built to connect the two units and for the current sanctuary space to be converted into an all-purpose space. The buildings were in need of considerable repair, and the small parking lot held only about 20 cars. The church had no building debt, however. Operating expenses ran about $200,000, and the church had a small building fund of about $150,000. Adjacent property had been available for purchase, but the cost was too high, because a developer was buying the surrounding property to build high-rise apartments.

Third Presbyterian had about 200 active members, including a large number of families with children. Average worship attendance was about 125. There was a part-time director of Christian education and a good Sunday school for all ages, as well as a strong music program with a half-time director who worked with an adult choir, a youth choir, and two choirs for children. The pastor of Third Presbyterian had been there over 10 years and wanted to return to the part of the United States where he grew up if an opportunity became available. He was well liked, and members were unaware of his desire to move.

In 1998, the church received a major gift of $2.5 million with no strings attached. The church had not made any decision on the use of the money at the time St. Paul approached them and invited them to consider merger. Several members knew each other from neighborhood and school activities. Two key members, one from each church, had worked together in city politics for several years and began to push for the merger.

The two churches agreed to explore possible merger and asked me to consult with them. Part of the one-year process they designed was to invite all members of each congregation to participate in a group interview process. One key question was, What interests or excites you about the possibilities of merger? The folks at St. Paul talked about having more people to carry out their mission and ministry, the possibility of attracting new people, especially young families with children for a Sunday school, and having a full-time pastor and perhaps a part-time education director. The major responses at Third Presbyterian were about better facilities, adequate parking, more service to the community, the option of using the endowment for mission instead of building, and the potential for growth with better facilities. It was apparent that there was enough common interest to proceed with moving toward a merger. Agreements reached in merger negotiations included:

- The church would be a union church and maintain relationships with both denominations.
- The congregation would be located at the site of St. Paul.
- A governing council would be made up of equal numbers from each congregation.

- The facilities of Third Presbyterian would be sold, with 50 percent of the proceeds to go to the presbytery and 50 percent to go into the endowment fund.
- The building fund of Third Presbyterian would be used to pay for some building improvements and remodeling at St. Paul.
- The endowment could not be drawn down below $2.5 million without full approval of the congregation. Interest and growth above that amount would be allocated as follows: 25 percent for unrestricted use in the operating budget, 25 percent for building maintenance or improvements, and 50 percent for mission projects.
- For a start-up period of three years, the congregation would be governed by a joint board. During that time, various organizational and mission structures would be tried, evaluated, and revised as needed.

The vision developed by the two congregations together is "to be a Union Church relating to both denominations, enabling people to grow in their understanding of the Christian Faith and serving the community through ministries of care and support."

Celebration

An important question to begin thinking about even during early discussions about a possible merger is, How will we celebrate the final result of the merger effort, regardless of the end result? The goal should be to recognize the members' learning and growth even if the more congregations cannot find a common vision and mission that will inspire and sustain them through a difficult period of transition and change.

When a merger does not come to fruition, one of the final steps should be to hold a service of worship to bring closure to the process. In this service, members are invited to express regrets, to ask forgiveness of each other if there has been hurt or pain, offer hope and encouragement, and ask God to bless each congregation as they continue their journeys of faith and service.

If the merger is completed and a new congregation is established, each congregation should hold a service of closing to lift up and celebrate past mission and ministry. The services should conclude with a movement to the site of the new congregation. Usually both congregations have a service of closure on the same day and then move together to mark the new start-up.

Merger as a new beginning can be a creative way to close congregations that are no longer viable or that are on a steady decline toward certain death. A merger, a true merger, can express the living reality of a resurrection faith. It can produce a new congregation that has the motivation and energy to carry out a new vision for God's mission and ministry in the world.

NOTE

1. Although there may be more than two congregations involved in a merger, to simplify communication, this chapter will assume there are only two.

7

A Judicatory Perspective

William Chris Hobgood

The middle judicatory can play an important role in the closing of a congregation. To understand this role, it is important to look first at what it means for a congregation to end its life.

The closing of the congregation becomes a possibility when leaders become so preoccupied with survival that there is little energy for anything else. In such times, focus on the present increases, because such enterprises seem relevant, in contrast to something so seemingly abstract as the future.

All of this attention on survival seems to seduce congregation members into an assumption that the congregation will always be around. I have talked with people who seemed insulted when I simply asked about their congregation's future. They responded: "Why would you ask? We will always be here. Now, let's get to work on our stewardship [or evangelism, or leadership, or whatever areas are problems for this congregation]."

From the perspective of this judicatory pastor, finally to close the book of a congregation's story is one of the most difficult and complex decisions any congregation can make. It is painful to admit, "We cannot go on any longer." For some people, closing a congregation means failure—that they have really let God down. No matter that God is more grace filled than we humans can ever comprehend; the congregation agonizes that with this closing they have failed in their duty to God.

On the other hand, members can make this decision to close in what seems a casual manner, as though the place is not worthy of deliberation. Such a "casual" closing usually comes about because it relieves members of what has become more of a burden than a place of joy. What seems to be a cavalier attitude can mask the denial that is part of deep grief.

However a congregation appears to approach the task, folding the congregational tent is never easy.

A Lot of Tents Are Folding

Several years ago Lyle Schaller, widely known church consultant and writer, said that between 50 and 60 Protestant congregations close each week in the United States. At first hearing, this might seem an absurdly high number. Yet consider some historical facts.

In the United States the westward movement of people of European ancestry was at its peak in the latter part of the 19th and early in the 20th centuries. During this time many, if not most, mainline congregations were established. In the early 1990s Bishop Richard Willke, who had oversight of two United Methodist conferences in Arkansas, told me that in the 19th century, the circuit riders planted churches within access of every person in the state. This meant a church could be reached after the chores were finished on a Sunday morning. At the time Willke was bishop there were, he said, 850 United Methodist congregations in Arkansas, and the majority had fewer than 50 members. Many of them would not merge or share a pastor with another small congregation. Many would have to close. But they would not face that reality. What was true of those Arkansas Methodists has been true of all mainline Protestants.

Willke's observations remind us that every congregation, like every person, goes through a life cycle. We can describe five stages in this life cycle:

1. Formation: the dream and dreamers are alive, and all who take part do so because they endorse the dream and want to be part of an exciting new venture.
2. Expansion: the congregation grows in many ways, including numerically, to reach a stable and healthy size.
3. Stabilization: the congregation is at its most productive regarding stewardship, leadership, program development, and in many other ways.
4. Breakdown: the dream is being forgotten, nostalgia for past glories becomes a most powerful force, and survival begins to claim the congregation's life.
5. Crisis: the life cycle ends, either in the congregation's death or its revitalization.[1]

Huge numbers of American congregations are now in the last two life-cycle stages, in part because of when they were founded. The question for these congregations, then, is not, "Should we feel bad because we are dying?" but "Because dying may be a normal part of our life, how should we go about doing it most faithfully?"

Enter the Judicatory

In an installation service for a judicatory pastor, the preacher named two basic functions of this office:

1. To be a sign of the unity and wholeness of the church. That is, to represent, to the congregation, the reality and joy that the church is far, far larger than what we see in this one place and time.

2. To be the pastor of the pastors.

   My understanding of this, as a judicatory pastor for 16 years, has been that I am to be "pastor to the relationship" of the pastor with her congregation. I count it very important that every pastor have pastoral care and will offer this if appropriate. At other times, I will see that pastors receive that care from others. I do not need to be every pastor's pastor. But I do believe my vocation is to give pastoral care to that critical relationship between pastor and congregation.

All of this means that the judicatory has a role in the end times of a congregation. In this pastoral role, judicatory staff can, at best, give guidance and support, and at least, offer understanding and empathy. Judicatory staff should be both caring and well informed.

The judicatory can also be an objective, corrective presence. This does not mean telling the congregation where it is wrong or right. Rather, it is about helping the congregation choose its direction. The judicatory should, gently if possible, always remind the congregation of its place in the whole story of God's people. From this perspective, judicatory staff offer the prophetic truth that none of us, individual or congregation, can stand alone— make decisions that do not take all other faithful people and communities into account.

A particular judicatory responsibility that comes to the fore at this time is its role as protector of the church. Congregations need protection from dangers within and without, self-inflicted or imposed by external forces and sources. When a congregation is fragile enough to be near its end, it may need protection from those outside who want the property or those inside who just want to avoid any responsibilities for the congregation's failing life. The judicatory, whether the denomination's polity gives it title to the property or the property is owned by the congregation, can be the place where the most alert watchfulness and protection is carried out.

The judicatory can also help congregations learn from the successes and mistakes of other congregations. Most congregations do not know how others have gone about closing. Judicatories, though, should have such a recorded memory and should be ready to share it when it is appropriate.

The Congregation Alone

"Incapable," "avoiding," and even "corrupt" are often some of the words that can describe the congregation that tries to settle its final affairs alone. Certainly there are congregations that have finished life well. But the danger is always present that issues of survival, an incomplete understanding of the options, and fear of the unknown will weigh so heavily on members that good decisions cannot be made.

In one situation, a congregation whose polity gave its members final authority to do so voted to close. Not wanting to consult the judicatory, they left the disposal of property in the hands of their trustees. All but one of the trustees said, in effect, that because the congregation's life was over, they could no longer function as trustees. Only one of the trustees stuck with it. She did not accept any help or counsel from the judicatory. Eventually she rented the space to a small new church but had absolutely no idea what would happen next. Legal wrangling ensued, and in time the case was adjudicated in court and the renting congregation was given title to the property. Because of bad decisions, that congregation was not able to commit its resources to carrying on the denomination's heritage in another location. The myth that "the denomination just wants to get its hands on our property" guided the congregation's decisions. The truth was, the judicatory did seek title. A handful of the leaders rejected this request, because they could not see a second truth: the property would have been used to further the mission of the church. The rest is history.

Sometimes decisions made in haste can result in property and other resources being lost and sacred trusts ignored or even abandoned. The promise of the congregation's legacy can die if, for example, the land and building go to the lowest bidder. (One talented artist in a congregation managed to frighten many members into taking responsible action by posting a drawing of the building with a fast food restaurant sign standing high above it.)

On the other hand, a decision to delay action as long as one member is around can be just as painful. Such avoidance may leave only a few people, perhaps old and disabled, with overwhelming responsibilities. It was at such a point—when only four aging women remained as members of First Faithful Church of Howville (Sunday school and worship had ceased some 10 years before)—that "the congregation" turned to the judicatory for help. Two of the women had been placed in medical institutions because of chronic illnesses. The other two simply decided to give the property to the judicatory. The cost to the judicatory for legal services was higher than what was received from the sale of their small building. Only giving the pews to a new church made this closure a time of hope rather than defeat.

Whether a congregation closes in haste or the closing is not recognized until long after the fact, thoughtful attention to the closing can result in the opportunity to pass on a legacy of hope for ministry in another place.

How Judicatories Can Help

Ideally, the judicatory has developed a strategy of preparing for and working with congregations as they near their end.

Some judicatories might take a hands-off approach, assuming that the congregation will make its decisions without assistance from the judicatory. This is more likely in polities where final authority lies within the congregation. But theoretically, even in Presbyterian or Episcopal polities, congregations can wait until they are virtually dead and then inform the presbytery or the bishop of the state of things. Unfortunately, this is probably the most common approach in all kinds of polities.

Far better is a partnership between the judicatory and congregations that can continue even if the congregation closes. It is true that a healthy relationship between these two expressions of the church needs to exist for far more reasons than the need to survive the end times. But if such a partnership has stood the challenges inherent even in healthy and happy times, that partnership can carry into these more painful times. Then if someone grumbles, "The judicatory just wants to get its hands on this property," someone else can reply, "Yes, they do, and for good reason: to further the church's mission."

For the church's mission to be furthered in such a time, the judicatory must prepare staff or consultants to work with identified dying congregations. It is best if the congregations themselves identify what is happening to them, but if a partnership exists, judicatory staff can help the congregation name this reality. Staff and consultants can help congregations explore their history, community demographics, mission needs and opportunities, and new congregation possibilities, so decisions may be made about the disposition of assets. Also, the judicatory can be of essential pastoral value in helping the members and their pastor spend time in prayer and reflection as they seek to discern their best courses of action. The congregation's ending may be identified early enough that the focus may even be placed on a redevelopment plan. Essential to this process, whatever the outcome, are three elements.

1. The judicatory can be the nonanxious presence in a situation often loaded with anxiety for clergy and members. This nonanxious presence can make it possible to ask objective questions, clarify necessary steps in ways that make them seem possible rather than overwhelming to pastor and members, and simply calm the atmosphere.

2. The judicatory can help the members explore their story, so they can see the power present in it but also discover whether the reason for their congregation's initial formation still exists or whether there are new reasons for the congregation to go on. From their story they can gain clues about how to dispose of tangible resources and at the same time celebrate the important ministries that happened in this place, through these people.

3. The judicatory can teach and preach God's truth that death is not an enemy, that indeed, life comes after death. For Christians, this is the essential truth of the good news. Why should this truth not be proclaimed when the ending of a congregation is immanent?

Two Cases

I want to offer two descriptions of judicatory-congregation partnership at a congregation's closing. From these we can then draw insights about ways for judicatory and congregation to work together.

The Wilmington Church

The Wilmington Church was established in the 1960s with great hope and promise, but its growth was stymied by great heartbreak. Located in a suburb of fast growing Wilmington, Delaware, everything seemed ideal. Expansion moved steadily upward, but then some unfortunate events took place, weakening trust and interrupting growth. In the life cycle described earlier, it was as though this congregation skipped "stabilization" and moved directly from "expansion" to "breakdown." Many members were lost, and at one point a division resulted in one-third of the congregation leaving.

Jim C's arrival as pastor in the early 1990s was an important step towards stability. Jim, though, saw early on that there was not a critical mass of members to carry out the congregation's ministry and mission. While giving fine pastoral care and excelling as preacher and leader of the whole congregation, Jim asked members whether they should continue life as a congregation.

For five years, the congregation chose not to struggle with this issue (denial). Finally, as a result of new responsibilities raised during a partnership dialogue with a congregation of another denomination, the people of Wilmington began to decide that they simply did not have the wherewithal to carry a fair share of this new load.

They entered a time of prayer and reflection, seeking to be honest about whether they had the community numbers and energy not just to survive, but to thrive. During this time, they asked the judicatory to work with them to explore their options.

The judicatory pastoral leader, its trustees, and the new congregation development team leader began working with Wilmington Church. The first task was to answer their questions about closing. Following this, the team worked to help them take the appropriate steps to carry out their decision to end their ministry.

The judicatory suggested that it was important that they not decide too quickly. They needed not only to pray, but also to talk with one another and the judicatory staff member and then discern, through their interaction, God's path for them. Their first inclination to close, which dated in part to Jim's first question, was confirmed.

At this point the judicatory began working with them to develop a closure strategy. The members did an inventory of resources. It was important that members, not the judicatory, do this. It helped members name what they would be offering up to the larger church. It was part of saying good-bye to their life together.

The inventory was shared with all congregations in the judicatory, and a bidding system established. First-come, first-served prevailed for most items. The judicatory pastor and a small team from the congregation determined the distribution of items of particular value, such as the handbells and the organ.

A decision needed to be made about the real property, the land and building. Wilmington had to decide whether they would manage the property sale or yield this to the judicatory. The land was still held by the judicatory, because it was a relatively new church (in congregational polity, the judicatory often holds title to land until the first mortgage is paid). The building, though, was owned by the congregation. A decision was made to give the title to the building to the judicatory as well. The congregation was asked to name its preferences for the disposal of funds from the sale of property. Although suggestions were made by the judicatory as needed, the congregation drew up the final list. The judicatory's trustees took care of an appraisal, engaging a real estate agent, selling the property, and disposing of the receipts per the congregation's desires.

A matter of great importance was the celebration of thanksgiving for Wilmington Church's life. A final worship experience, including releasing balloons and other festive symbols of continuing life, affirmed both the congregation's decision to close and its decisions about continuing its mission through a new congregation and the larger church's mission.

Finally, the members of the Wilmington Church were carried on the rolls of the judicatory as members-at-large until they had found new church homes. Their pastor was invited to found a new congregation near Wilmington, and this he did until retirement. Closure was faithfully accomplished, in large part because the judicatory had a strategy for such times that was firmly and gently applied.

Wilhelm Park Church

Wilhelm Park Church had worked for over 80 years in south Baltimore, never becoming large, but always seeking to be faithful to its call as a congregation-centered "free church." It was located on a side street in a predominately Roman Catholic neighborhood. Baltimore has been described as the southernmost of the great northeastern cities, abounding in ethnic neighborhoods. "A city of towns" was the way one native described her city.

Wilhelm Park Church was started in 1919 at the initiative of another congregation in the city. Several founding members came from the parent church, and a lay preacher offered the first pastoral leadership. The congregation settled into a comfortable size of 50 to 75 members. Land had been purchased from the local stockyards as they sought to dispose of their properties when their business began declining. The congregation built a sanctuary first and many years later built a detached fellowship building. No one could later remember why the two buildings were not connected, except that it may have been less costly to do it this way.

A paired relationship was established with another small congregation in the 1970s. For 25 years this arrangement offered one full-time pastor to both congregations, with a minimum of schedule adjustment for worship, given that the two were only four miles apart.

In the late 1990s, as numbers declined and members aged, attempts were made to adjust the relationships between the two churches. Wilhelm Park was less able to give its fair share as its resources diminished. The partner congregation raised understandable questions about continuing the relationship.

Finally, with but five regular participants remaining, Wilhelm Park met with a judicatory pastor to begin discussions about closing. It helped that the congregation had a good, trusting relationship with the judicatory, so this was not just the beginning of a friendship. Issues such as making a prayerful, faithful, and final decision; selling and disposing of real and other properties; organizing a closing celebration; and determining the future of the few remaining members were discussed, and decisions made over a period of several months.

The final decision was to turn over the title for all real property to the judicatory for sale. Recommendations were also made for the disposition of funds received from the sale of property. It was Wilhelm Park's expressed desire that two congregations benefit from its stewardship. One would purchase their building, and a second new church would be established at some time in the future in Baltimore. The building was sold to a congregation with limited resources that would have had difficulty developing its own space otherwise, and funds received from that sale went to several mission-centered purposes, particularly for the new congregation project.

Other possessions of the congregation were donated to small and new churches. Some items were sold, and receipts were used for final costs and gifts to the pastor and organist. One important arrangement was that the shared pastor continued to receive Wilhelm Park's portion of his compensation until his retirement, which had already been set for three months after the congregation's closing.

As with Wilmington, a season of prayer preceded these final acts, and a closing celebration drew many former members and offered a clean, hope-centered end to their story.

None of their decisions could have been made so clearly had the congregation not had a trusted ally in the judicatory staff. That staff provided pastoral and practical counsel to them throughout their final months, gave pastoral leadership in their closing celebration, and made certain that their decisions about disposition of assets were followed.

Essential Steps and Polity Variations

From these and other experiences, we can identify three essential parts of the judicatory's relationship to the congregation: pastoral, practical, and spiritual.

The first is pastoral. The judicatory can be very helpful as a pastoral presence while the members of a congregation come to terms with their situation. The congregation is going through a grieving process, and the support, understanding, and counsel of a caring pastor can make grief more bearable. Years ago, Elizabeth Kübler-Ross identified five stages that are in varying degrees present in all grieving processes: denial, anger, bargaining, depression, and acceptance.[2] It has been my experience that all of these stages unfold during the congregation's decision to close. If it is going to end with hope, it is important that those with the responsibility for pastoral oversight assist the congregation in grieving. Just to name these stages as normal and not bizarre can help. The practice of prayer and discernment can be immensely healing as denial and anger begin to take place, and sometimes it is the somewhat removed pastoral friend who can help this happen.

The second part of the judicatory's role is practical. Members trying to help a congregation close are often faced with overwhelming questions and no answers. Whatever the polity, the matter of disposition of the congregation's real and other tangible property is the largest unknown. Even a congregation's trustees usually have not a clue about such matters. This is why it serves a judicatory well to have either a special task force or a standing group charged with the task of gathering information so that the members will hear wise and accurate answers to their myriad questions. The judicatory can help by developing guidelines for congregational closings. These should reflect the denomination's polity, the judicatory's particular emphases (such as committing resources to new congregation establishment), as well as broader ideas about process such as those noted above.

In polities where title to property is not held by the congregation and the final decision about closure and disposition of property is not in the hands of the congregation, by established procedure a person, committee, or team will be named to assist in this process. In the Presbyterian Church (U.S.A.), for example, the congregation's presbytery will name an administrative commission, which will work with the congregation in legal, ecclesial, and spiritual matters related to the closing.

The third critical part of this relationship is spiritual. This is the context in which the closure events are planned and carried out and the congregation's life is brought to an end. Specific plans need to be developed for closing events, assuring the pastoral care of members after the closing, and making certain that the members who gave of their best at the end are included in decisions about use of the resources that remain.

Some Important Lessons

I believe there are at least four lessons to be learned from the congregational endings I have witnessed.

First, *don't wait too long, or it will be too late*; too late, that is, for a closure that will be managed faithfully while giving appropriate and needed pastoral care to members. Those grief stages listed earlier can sometimes be detected years before the end. For example, denial can cause many a congregation member to refuse to face the reality of its decline. Anger can create barriers between the congregation and the judicatory that prevent good decision making. Depression can immobilize a congregation just when it most needs to be alert and constructive in its planning. It is vital that the judicatory help congregations see the whole span of their lives and to identify the movements of the life cycle early enough to live them in healthy ways, without feeling like they have done something wrong when the end is nearing.

Second, *never give up hope for possibilities*. At times the very act of recognizing denial for what it is will help a congregation take seriously the need to undergo revitalizing change. But if rebirth is not possible, faithful hope can make the closing of the congregation's life a song of celebration rather than a dirge. If the whole church ever runs out of ministries to be carried out, then we can sing a sad song, but until then, this congregation's resources, the faithful energies of members, the stories of devoted service that took place here, can always be transformed into new, life-giving ministries, perhaps in other places.

Third, *be willing to change, especially in death*. According to the Christian gospel, death is the greatest of change-events. And that means positive change. Why should the congregation's death be any different? The few remaining members of the Wilhelm Park Church were moved beyond words when they realized that their ending would result in at least two new ministries. A struggling ethnic minority congregation found a lease on life by purchasing the property for one, and the income from that sale went to establish another new congregation of Wilhelm Park's denomination. This was the single greatest act of witness in this congregation's history.

Finally, *believe that death and life are both as natural to congregations as they are to us as individuals*. Christians proclaim that life comes after death, not before it. Again, why should the end of a congregation's life be viewed any differently? It is when we hold to the conviction that God gives life after death that we can see our shared life ending with hope.

NOTES

1. Lawrence Cada, Raymond Fitz, Gertrude Foley, Thomas Giardino, and Carol Lichtenberg, *Shaping the Coming Age of Religious Life* (New York: Seabury, 1979), 53–61.

2. Elizabeth Kübler-Ross, *On Death and Dying* (New York: Collier Books, 1997).

PART 2

Stories about Closings

8

A Tale of Two Closings

Lindsay Louise Biddle

Both churches had experienced the best of times and the worst of times, and both churches closed. One died with thanksgiving, joy, and hope. The other went to its grave conflicted and burned out.

Scots' Memorial–Lakewood Presbyterian Church was the result of a merger in the early 1970s. Scots' Memorial Presbyterian Church had been founded in the late 19th century by Scottish immigrants to Saint Paul, Minnesota. During its first 50 years the church operated an English language school for immigrants of various European nationalities. After the Second World War, the school became an independent language arts college. The congregation's membership peaked at over 1,000 in the early 1960s before steadily dropping. Church leaders attributed the decline to "the changing neighborhood"; that is, the influx of newer, non-European immigrants and people of color. This was due primarily to the city's repeal of laws that had kept real estate in the hands of whites, the nearby construction of an interstate highway that lowered real estate values, and the ensuing "white flight" to the suburbs.

Lakewood Presbyterian Church began as a mission post in "rural" south Minneapolis in the 1900s. Chartered by members from the Downtown United Presbyterian Church, it was part of the presbytery's goal at the turn of the century "that no geographical portion of the city be devoid of the true Reformed faith and spiritual wisdom of John Calvin." Built on a bluff overlooking the Mississippi River that separates the Twin Cities, Lakewood was very supportive of global missions. It took great pride in the number of missionaries it produced, including the first missionary to serve as moderator of the denomination's general assembly. By 1970, the neighborhood had become predominantly Jewish, and the congregation split over whether and how to proselytize in the community. At the eye of the storm was the pastor, who had grown up in the church. He married one of his converts, a woman from a prominent Jewish family, and they abruptly left to start a Christian commune in Iowa, taking most of the younger members with them.

With its membership rolls depleted by conflict, Lakewood quickly accepted Scots' Memorial's proposal to merge the congregations. Scots' Memorial was interested in relocating to a new area, and Lakewood needed all the members it could get, so members decided to sell the Scots' Memorial building in Saint Paul and keep Lakewood's building in Minneapolis. With Lakewood's pastor already gone, the newly merged congregation was served by the pastor of Scots' Memorial until his retirement in 1978.

The search for a new minister brought out key differences among the members of Scots' Memorial–Lakewood Presbyterian Church. Over the next two decades a series of pastors tried their best to help the congregation grow spiritually as well as numerically. Various programs were initiated, projects undertaken, and studies conducted. Fund-raisers were held every year to help balance the church's budget. The session considered holding a capital improvements campaign in conjunction with the 100th anniversary of the founding of Scots' Memorial, but leaders could not agree on whether to use the money to develop off-street parking or make the church building handicap accessible. Also, it was rumored that some Lakewood folks would not participate in a celebration that honored only Scots' Memorial. Meanwhile, the congregation lost many more members than it took in. The budget shrank, programs fell by the wayside, and no one pastor stayed for more than four years.

By 1998, the church had dropped to less than 150 members. The presbytery appointed a part-time pastor to serve the congregation and help the session devise a redevelopment strategy. On her first Sunday, the pastor noticed two different sets of trays and cups on the communion table. After a few weeks, she realized that the former members of Scots' Memorial sat on one side of the sanctuary, the former members of Lakewood sat on the other, and each group used the communion set from its former church. Anyone who had joined the church since the merger in 1978 was considered "new."

The pastor also noticed that only two of the six session members attended worship regularly. Two others, a husband and wife, went to visit her mother in a nursing home every Sunday. The clerk and the treasurer spent Sunday mornings in the church office paying bills, typing reports, and—after the offering was received during worship—counting and recording the money. When the pastor encouraged them to take Sunday off from business in honor of the Sabbath and for their own spiritual well-being, the treasurer got defensive and threatened to quit. The clerk explained that he worshiped at his daughter's church during the week and continued to serve as clerk because no one else was willing to do it.

After a Sudanese family attended worship once, the pastor overheard a member ask, "Who were those nice colored people? I hope they come back."

At the pastor's suggestion, the session sponsored a congregational forum to brainstorm ideas for redevelopment. A member of the presbytery's committee on church growth agreed to facilitate the discussion. One member suggested hosting an event for neighborhood youth so as to attract their families, but another member cited "the hard work we put into years of vacation Bible schools only to have all these kids running around making messes in our church, and their parents never darkened the door." The facilitator pushed the group to define their current mission, they developed a thoughtful statement with three points, and they voted unanimously for the session to explore ways of implementing the statement and report back to the congregation. Everyone felt the forum was a success and time well spent.

At the next session meeting, the pastor attempted to lead the elders in an exercise to envision ways of putting the new mission statement into practice. "I thought that's what we're paying *you* for," responded one elder. "Isn't that why the presbytery sent you here?" The pastor took that as a cue to offer some of her own ideas, but each one was shot down in turn. "We're already doing all we can," said another elder. When pressed to think of one new action that might make a significant difference in the life of the congregation, the session was at a loss. The pastor left the meeting feeling frustrated and discouraged. She resigned at the end of the year to take another position.

For the next six months, a string of guest preachers supplied the church's pulpit on Sunday mornings, and a member of the presbytery's committee on ministry led the session in conducting their regular business and discussing their future. A former Lakewood member insisted that the church stay open long enough to celebrate Lakewood's 100th anniversary in 2002, "since the other church got to celebrate theirs." After considerable debate, someone checked the historical records and reported that Lakewood had actually held its first worship service in January 1900, even though it was not officially chartered until its building was completed in 1902. With this new information, the session recommended to the congregation and to the presbytery that Scots' Memorial–Lakewood Presbyterian Church close in January 2000.

The presbytery approved the decision and established an administrative commission to carry out the tasks of dissolving the church as an incorporated, religious, nonprofit organization. The commission included ministers and elders from other churches in the presbytery, as well as two elders from the congregation: one from Scots' Memorial and the other from Lakewood. In consultation with the congregation, the commission decided to sell the church building to the highest bidder. After donating the liturgical furnishings to other congregations, the other furnishings were inventoried as to where they came from and auctioned accordingly. Things from Lakewood were offered to those members, things from Scots' Memorial were offered to them, and new members were offered everything else. All the proceeds were similarly divided: a third went to the language arts college begun by Scots' Memorial, a third went to foreign missions in honor of Lakewood's 100th anniversary, and a third went to the presbytery's fund for new church development.

During the closing service of worship, the history of each congregation was highlighted. A retired missionary who had grown up in the Lakewood Church preached the final sermon; all the pastors who had served Scots' Memorial had died by this time. Upon dissolution, everyone's membership was transferred to the presbytery until they joined other churches. Some people immediately joined Presbyterian churches, a few chose non-Presbyterian churches attended by family members or closer to home, but the rest were never heard from again.

Omega Presbyterian Church was started during the Great Depression in the 1930s by a minister who had been raised in the slums of New York City and was committed to social ministry among the poor and disenfranchised. The congregation began with a few families and individuals meeting in the pastor's home in east Minneapolis each week for worship, Bible study, and a meal. When the group outgrew the pastor's house, they took it upon themselves to acquire a run-down Victorian-style mansion. Some of the men were out-of-work craftsmen, and they renovated the mansion and used it as an opportunity to teach their skills to the younger people. During the war years, when most of the men were away, the group continued to grow by taking in destitute families and helping them find adequate housing, jobs, and schools.

After the war the pastor and his flock petitioned the presbytery to issue them a charter as a Presbyterian Church. The presbytery did so on the condition that the congregation would present plans for a church building within a year. On Easter Sunday in 1946, as part of a worship service held outdoors in a city park, Omega Presbyterian Church was officially organized. The congregation drew its name from the last letter of the Greek alphabet to reflect the words of Jesus in the Gospel of Mark: "But many that are first will be last, and the last first" (10:31 RSV). The pastor preached on the story of the rich man who asked what he must do to inherit eternal life. "Go, sell what you have, and give to the poor, and you will have treasure in heaven; and come, follow me' " (Mark 10:21 RSV). This verse was adopted as the first mission statement of the new church.

The congregation never built a building. This was primarily due to their sense of priorities and partly due to the opportunities that came along. In 1947, they purchased an abandoned warehouse and, again, used the renovation to do ministry. By this time they had outgrown the mansion, so it was converted into housing for poor families. The pastor left to go work for an ecumenical aid agency back East, and the congregation became intentional about calling second-career ministers who had different life experiences. Throughout the 1950s and '60s, they met in the former warehouse where they also sponsored a theater group, a job training program, and one of the first day-care centers in the city.

During the 1970s and '80s, Omega's membership declined slightly while the needs of the community skyrocketed. Then the AIDS epidemic hit, and the church, once again, altered its space to meet new needs. The mansion became one of the first group homes for people in the final stages of illness related to HIV/AIDS, and a meals-on-wheels program was started in the warehouse. In 1996, the city asked Omega to join a metrowide initiative to address the emerging needs of non-English speaking residents. The congregation was seeking a minister at the time, so they extended the search to find someone who spoke Spanish. Meanwhile, some of the members and the interim pastor immersed themselves in the neighboring Latino community. After two years of concerted effort, however, they were still without sufficient programs or a new pastor.

The congregation regularly met during the week for worship, a meal, and Bible study, and they began to invite members of the Latino community to join them. In 1998, the interim pastor suggested that during Lent they engage in an intentional listening process, using the five interim tasks, to help discern what God was calling them to next.[1] Cofacilitated by a teacher of English as a second language who was Latino, and by the interim pastor, a Hungarian American who was learning Spanish as a third language, they sang praise songs in both Spanish and English and ate supper together. Then everyone mixed in small groups to read scripture aloud in both languages and, after a brief silence, discuss personally and confidentially what the verses meant to each person.

WEEK ONE
> What is my story? What is my history?
>>   Psalm 33, A hymn to the God of history

WEEK TWO
> Who am I? How do I identify myself?
>>   Luke 9:18-20, Who do you say Jesus is?

WEEK THREE
> What changes do I want to make?
>>   Mark 7:24-30, Jesus' ministry shifts

WEEK FOUR
> Who do I depend on? Who depends on me?
>>   The story of Ruth

WEEK FIVE
> What do you want Jesus to do for you?
>>   Mark 10:46-52, Blind Bartimaeus

The conversations began politely and cautiously but over time became more heartfelt and honest. They continued past Lent and into the Easter season, raising more questions than they answered. One Anglo member of the congregation admitted having his eyes opened for the first time to the daily discrimination encountered by members of his group. Several members of the Latino community confessed that although they appreciated everything that others did for them, they needed their own space and autonomy.

Later that spring the session went on its annual retreat. They focused on Omega's original mission statement, and they paid particular attention to the story of blind Bartimaeus (Mark 10:46-52). In response to Jesus' question to Bartimaeus, "What do you want me to do for you?" the elders sat in silence for over an hour. Finally someone ventured to say, "I believe we are like this blind man wanting to see again, wanting some direction. And the needs of the community are telling us, 'Take heart; get up, Jesus is calling you.' Perhaps a new vision is staring us in the face and we need to move on." Another elder responded, "This congregation has always been about giving to those in need so they might take charge of their own lives. We've seen a lot of people come and go, and they've usually left better off than they came. Maybe it's time for us to go. We're certainly better off now than our forebears were during the Depression." The interim pastor chimed in, "I dare to say this as a member of the institutional church but, regardless of how much ownership we take, it's never *our* church. The church doesn't belong to its members—the members belong to the church of Jesus Christ." Then with tears in her eyes, another elder said, "As much as I've enjoyed all that we've done over the years, I now feel *our* doing is getting in the way of others doing for themselves. It's like turning the family business over to your children. It's difficult but necessary if the work is going to continue to grow and serve their needs like it did yours."

The session soon held a forum with the congregation, now fewer than 100 members, during which they described what had happened on the retreat. They asked the congregation to prayerfully consider closing the church as it was currently organized in order that it might be started anew by a congregation more representative of the community. They also asked the presbytery's permission to put the church's search for a new pastor on hold and explained the reason why.

The session expected some resistance from members and even some second thoughts from among themselves. What they did not count on was the response of some leaders in the presbytery. One minister passed around a petition ordering the session of Omega to be disbanded "for obvious lack of faith." The presbytery's committee on church growth was said to be against any closings in the middle of their campaign to get "2,000 new members by the year 2000." The presbytery held a special meeting with the session during which an elder from Omega countered, "Wouldn't it be nice if some of those 2,000 new members were Latinos?"

Finally in early 1999, with the blessing of its committee on church growth and committee on ministry, the presbytery approved a series of consultation meetings involving members of Omega, the Latino community, the presbytery, and the denominational staff for Latino ministries in the United States. The warehouse was by now in need of repair, and the group recommended that a grant from the denomination be used to make the building livable for the next organizers. Building inspections determined, however, that the warehouse needed to be razed. Thus the grant money was used to purchase building materials, and volunteers from the community and other churches provided the supervision and labor to erect a new structure.

With the building project estimated to be finished by early 2001, the decision was made to close Omega Presbyterian Church on Easter Sunday 2001, exactly 55 years after it was chartered. Someone found a stack of old bumper stickers from the state's department of transportation that said "Arrive Alive at 55!" and plastered them around the work site. The presbytery established an administrative commission to carry out the work of officially dissolving the congregation. Members of the Latino community were invited to meet with the commission to decide what furnishings to keep and what to donate. The commission in consultation with the congregation and community accepted a health organization's offer to purchase the mansion and continue to operate it as a care facility for low-income people with terminal illnesses.

Members of Omega continued to meet together during the week and were served by their interim pastor. On Sunday mornings they began attending worship at other churches in the presbytery. Sometimes they were asked to share their experiences with a Sunday school class. Meanwhile the presbytery searched for a Latino pastor to serve as a new church developer.

Easter 2001 finally arrived, and, to no one's surprise, the new building was still under construction. So, in the same city park where the congregation had been chartered over half a century ago, the members of Omega Presbyterian Church gathered for their final service of worship. They were joined by folks from the community, the presbytery, and the building project, as well as former members. The congregation sang hymns of resurrection, both in Spanish and in English, and the interim pastor preached, also in both languages, about the church of Jesus Christ being a temporary organization—formed, reformed, and always reforming. She quoted from the Presbyterian Book of Order, "The Church is called to undertake [its] mission even at the risk of losing its life, trusting in God alone as the author and giver of life, sharing the gospel, and doing those deeds in the world that point beyond themselves to the new reality in Christ."[2]

After giving thanks for the church's ministry, the moderator of the presbytery recalled the presbytery's decision back in 1946 to charter this congregation on the condition that they build a building. "It's about time!" he said, and everyone laughed. Some carpenters from the congregation had carved omegas out of wood taken from the warehouse and gave one to each person present. Then members of the Latino community gathered hands around the whole congregation and sang,

> *Pues si vivimos para Él vivimos, y si morimos para Él morimos.*
> *Sea que vivamos o que muramos, Somos del Señor, semos del*
> *Señor.*
> When we are living, it is in Christ Jesus, and when we're dying, it
> is in the Lord.
> Both in our living and in our dying, we belong to God, we belong to
> God.[3]

Following the service, the Latino community hosted a traditional feast for everyone. Realizing this was a unique closing, the presbytery called the interim pastor to continue serving the spiritual needs of the former members and to assist them in joining other congregations. By the beginning of the next fall, they all had transferred their memberships to other churches. To this day they meet every month for Bible study and a meal.

The presbytery called a Puerto Rican-born Presbyterian minister to organize a Latino congregation. Interestingly, he had grown up in the same area of New York City as the organizing pastor of the Omega church. The worshiping community calls itself "Pueblo nuevo en el amor" or "new people bound by love."[4] The new building is being used for ministry even as it is being completed. Pueblo Nuevo Presbyterian Church expects to charter with over 200 members.

NOTES

1. For more information on interim ministry and the five interim tasks, contact the Interim Ministry Network, 5740 Executive Drive, Suite 220, Baltimore, Maryland 21228; telephone: 800-235-8414; fax: 410-719-0795; e-mail: info@interimministry.org; Web site: www.interimministry.org. For more about integrating personal faith, corporate discernment, and congregational life, see *Spiritual Awakening: A Guide to Spiritual Life in Congregations* (Bethesda, Md.: The Alban Institute, 1994) and *Listening to God: Spiritual Formation in Congregations* (Bethesda, Md.: The Alban Institute, 2001), both by John Ackerman.

2. From Chapter III, "The Church and Its Mission," Section G-3.0400 of the Constitution of the Presbyterian Church (U.S.A.) Part II Book of Order (Louisville, Ky.: Office of the General Assembly, 2001).

3. From the hymn, "Pues Si Vivimos" or "When We Are Living," a Spanish melody. Stanza 1 is translated by Elise S. Eslinger, 1983, from *The Presbyterian Hymnal* (Louisville, Ky.: Westminster/John Knox Press, 1990), no. 400.

4. From the hymn, "Una Espiga" or "Sheaves of Summer" by Cesáreo Gabaráin, 1973, translated by George Lockwood, 1988, and harmony by Skinner Chávez-Melo, 1987, from *The Presbyterian Hymnal* (Louisville, Ky.: Westminster/John Knox Press, 1990), no. 518.

9

Closing Rural Congregations

Len Eberhart

Geography played an important part in establishing churches in rural Midwestern America. As communities were being established, it was determined that a farmer could reasonably travel seven miles to town to conduct business after morning chores were done and still get back in time for evening chores. So, many towns, especially along railroad lines, were built about 14 miles apart. It seems a similar logic was applied to the establishment of churches. The landscape of rural America has changed dramatically in the last several decades, however. Demographic shifts from rural to urban are leaving a significant imprint. Whole towns have disappeared. Schools have been consolidated, usually accompanied by a great sense of loss. The church is one of the last institutions to which folks turn for grounding on what they expect to be a changeless, bedrock foundation. So when any mention is made in rural communities of entering into some sort of shared ministry or closing of a church, many past experiences contribute to the difficult feelings accompanying such consideration.

Finances are not often the primary problem in smaller congregations, because the remaining members are older, loyal, committed persons who will see to it that the necessary funding is available. More often the biggest problem is having a critical mass of people to carry on meaningful ministry. The beginning of decline is marked by the discontinuation of the Sunday school for children and youth. The final need members of a rural congregation have is for a chapel in which funeral services for the remaining members can be conducted.

Many rural communities in the Midwest have experienced the dramatic impact of the population shift in recent decades. The number of single-farm families who need to subsidize their income with off-farm employment is on the rise, so families move into town. Agriculture is becoming increasingly mechanized, so youth and young adults must find work elsewhere. In some states population has declined because Midwesterners are often sought after for their good work ethic and are recruited by employers elsewhere in the country.

Even while experiencing an exodus of the indigenous population, Iowa is experiencing an influx of new ethnic groups. The impact on the church is significant. Some of the new ethnic populations have settled in smaller rural communities, because housing and overall cost of living is lower there. The United Methodist Church in Iowa is attempting to create a hospitable environment for these new neighbors. The change in attitude needed to implement this welcome, however, is a stretch for congregations just hanging on for survival. Folks who lament over children leaving their communities have difficulty seeing the blessing in the arrival of a new neighbor who eats different foods, practices different customs, and speaks a different language.

Here in Iowa, we will likely never need all the rural congregations that have been established in the state over the decades. We do experience an opportunity to expand ministry to an increasingly diverse population, however. This is the context in which we are closing churches.

Castalia United Methodist Church

My first charge conference[1] as district superintendent was to conduct the annual business for Castalia United Methodist Church in October 1997. This single-point congregation had been served by a retired pastor since September 1992. I preached at the morning worship service. All the members, 12 people (the youngest of whom was in the upper 60s), were present at worship and the conference that followed a potluck lunch. Like many rural churches in Iowa, this congregation fits the description of a "cat-like" church—independent, possessing a high degree of self-determination, not easily dissuaded, wary of institutional structures and representatives. Still, the members were eager to meet this new district superintendent (DS).They were also cautious about dealing with an institutional bureaucrat, because they already knew how precarious their circumstance was but were just not able to face it. In subsequent conversations with the pastor, I asked about the mixed signals I was getting. He began to tell me about how they often did not meet every week, especially in winter. The majority of the regulars commuted from the countryside and other nearby communities.

My predecessor had been in consultation with the congregation the year before, coaching them on ways they could create a vision for revitalizing their ministry. He recommended they bring in a conference program staff person to assist them in this exploration. None of these suggestions were pursued. It may well have appeared to be too late for any meaningful intervention. My theme in each conversation with the congregation was focused on vital ministry. I told them the annual conference's objective is to support congregations in a ministry that makes a difference to people. When a church feels it no longer has the critical mass and resources to do this, then members need to decide when they should begin to take steps to close the church.

Because the pastor was willing to continue serving in this setting until the folks were ready to close, I did not press the congregation to make a decision. I provided information they requested about how they could bring the life of the congregation to a conclusion. In the spring of 2000 the pastor called to tell me that the congregation had made a decision that they were ready to formally close. They had not met for worship for almost a year, even on important days like Easter. They had met occasionally in a member's house. The pastor and I, along with four remaining members, met in a charge conference on June 12, 2000, to officially conclude the ministry of the church. Many of the furnishings had already been sold, given to other churches, or claimed by members of the church. Arrangements were being made to remove all of the religious symbols, including the bell from the tower. Negotiations were underway to transfer the church building to Habitat for Humanity, which would rehabilitate it into a single-family dwelling. Because the congregation did not want to have a concluding service of worship, I incorporated in the charge conference proceedings a time of reflection, recollection of memories, and affirmation of the nearly 150 years of ministry.

Many of the church records had been lost, but the pastor and several members reconstructed a membership list for the DS to use when carrying out the responsibilities for closing a church outlined in the United Methodist Book of Discipline. Those responsibilities include the following:[2]

A. The district building and location committee (which has responsibilities similar to a board of trustees) make a site visit. They ask two basic questions, among others:

      1. How will the ministry to this area be affected by taking this step?

      2. What are the plans for disposal of the property?

B. The appointive cabinet (12 district superintendents and the bishop) give their support to closing this church.

C. The pastor and superintendent each submit a letter concurring with this action.

D. The congregation convenes a properly called church conference to act on a recommendation to close the church.

E. The local church board of trustees is empowered to continue acting on behalf of the closed church to carry out directions for disposition of property and other assets. These actions are to be done in a timely manner.

F. The DS communicates the action to close the church in writing to all the members, lets them know where their membership will be lodged, and explains the process for transferring elsewhere if desired.

Once the DS had completed this final task, Castalia United Methodist Church was officially closed.

Murphy United Methodist

Murphy was one of three small congregations in a parish served by a pastor on a half-time basis. This congregation also had "cat-like" qualities. While membership and worship attendance had been in the single digits for some time, there were a few members who wanted this church to be the place where family and friends gathered to celebrate their resurrection when they died. The setting is a beautiful, idyllic, open-country spot surrounded with trees, lush lawn, and a cemetery. It is not hard to understand why a church was built on this spot. Although the property had been maintained, it did not have any water or sewer utilities. It did have electrical power.

During my time on the district staff, I had several conversations with this congregation. In July 1999, the half-time pastor moved. In anticipation of this change I entered into conversations with the three churches in the parish and adjoining congregations to explore options for future ministry. For a time this dialogue was hindered because of a misconception that the annual conference "owns" all property (as opposed to holding all property in trust).[3] There was no room in the minds of some members at Murphy to consider closing because the annual conference would "get the property." In the midst of these conversations, one Murphy member who wanted to help the process move along said to me, "I'll give you a hundred dollars for the church, and we'll call it even." We were eventually able to help people understand the distinction between owning and holding in trust.

A neighboring three-point parish being served by a full-time elder needed to cuts its expenses. One way to do this was to decrease staff. The option finally agreed upon was for the six churches to form a parish served by a full-time pastor and a certified lay speaker. The new parish alignment did not change the dynamics of the Murphy congregation. Two years later, the congregation made a decision to close. The timing of the decision to proceed with closing was likely precipitated by the sudden death of a pillar in the congregation who had opposed closing because he believed the annual conference would receive or take the property.

A church conference was convened on June 18, 2001, to formally close the church. Seven people, in addition to the pastor, were present. The elected trustees were empowered to pursue disposition of the property with a goal of having this task completed by September. Options under consideration included:

1. developing a fund to maintain the site as a local chapel (this was especially appealing to several elderly members who wanted to have their funerals held there)
2. selling or transferring the property to a private owner for use as a wedding chapel
3. razing the building, if no other options were possible

The congregation offered to honor its share of the pastoral support and parish expenses through the remainder of the calendar year. Any other remaining financial assets would be given to support ministries in the area. The charge conference action was to proceed with the usual protocol for taking this step.

The Murphy congregation, like the Castalia Church, did not want to hold a concluding worship. In both cases, it seemed the congregations had waited so long to decide to close that the critical mass of people was too small (a number of the members were not able to go out into public any longer). I believe another factor was at work: a significant degree of denial. People were simply unable to engage in this sort of life liturgy. Perhaps they were also exhibiting the dominant thread of stoicism so common among many rural folks. This trait prompts people to "bear it" without a great deal of outward emotion. Grief is often inwardly directed and expressed quietly among these folks, who are predominantly of northern European extraction. Many members might also have felt that by participating in a community liturgy to conclude the life of the congregation, they were participating in "churchicide."

Miles United Methodist Church

The Miles congregation was part of a three-point parish served by a full-time pastor, although the parish has had a variety of leaders, including seminary students, over the years. The parish was also once part of a seven-congregation parish that shared an educator. The Miles Church was the smallest of the three in the current parish (including about 20 percent of the parish members) and was located in the center of the parish along Highway 64. The Sabula congregation is located eight miles east of Miles on the Mississippi River. The Preston Church is four miles west of Miles. The largest community in the region is Maquokota, 13 miles west of Preston. The new north-south, four-lane Highway 61, just outside Maquokota and perpendicular to Route 64, was completed in 1999. The highway has spurred new industry in Maquoketa, and it is expected that in the near future these smaller communities will increasingly become bedroom communities.

This parish has experienced the effects of rural-to-urban population shift. Because of the growth in tourism along the Mississippi River on the eastern edge and the expansion of Highway 61 on the west edge of the parish, there clearly is potential for new ministry. The question of how many ministry sites are needed, however, raises several factors:

1. What is the population density, and what ministry niches is a specific congregation uniquely poised to address?
2. What geographical factors affect the situation? The topography along parts of the Mississippi River makes it difficult to get from point A to point B in a straight line. So part of the consideration about where to maintain ministry centers has to do with accessibility.

The logic used to plot the original communities seven miles apart is still a predominant factor in decisions about continuing churches.[4]

3. What is the level of energy and passion for ministry beyond caring for the members?

In virtually all of the conversations I had at Miles, one of the pillars of the congregation raised the question regarding viability of the church. At first he was more tentative, then he became adamant that the church needed to close. His argument was that Miles did not have the critical mass of people and resources to maintain a viable congregation. The attitude there seemed to be focused on how to be faithful rather than how to survive for as long as possible. I was asked to come to a meeting on January 31, 2000, to discuss options for the future of the church and followed my usual approach to help them exercise as much self-determination as possible. At one point near the end of the evening, one woman somewhat exasperatedly said, "Why don't you just tell us what to do!" I paused a moment and then responded, "Okay. I'd like you to spend the next 30 days in a prayerful reading and discussion of Acts. Pay particular attention to what gave meaning to the early church and the participation of those early members in ministry." Needless to say, it was not the answer she expected or wanted.

The pastor reported that he did a sermon series on Acts for the next month. Some groups did spend time in study and conversation. I was asked to come back on May 23, 2000. I brought Jill S., a staff member,[5] with me. We again worked hard to help the congregation think about options rather than focusing on the dire financial concerns that required closing the church. Then in the middle of the meeting it seemed as if a 180-degree turn occurred. Several people commented that it would be interesting to find out a little more about the demographic makeup of the parish. The pastor suggested that they might do surveys in each of the three towns, including the other churches in those communities, so that the study would be a community endeavor rather than the effort of just one denomination. Before we knew it, there was a fairly substantial consensus to move in this direction. We left the evening session with the pastor volunteering to explore the interest among the other denominational leaders in each of the three towns. There were several members who said they would be willing to work on a task force to help put together a process for evaluating demographic data from Percept, available through the Iowa Annual Conference's contract with the organization, and help design a way to do further canvassing in the communities. Jill and I agreed that we would find a way to fund Percept's gathering of more detailed information.

The pastor agreed to get back with us once he had opportunity to canvas the other clergy in the communities and then invite Jill to help them formulate the next steps of the process. The evening ended on a much more invigorating note than when we began the session and was certainly much more upbeat than the previous conversations we had held in this parish. The conversations moved the congregation to invite people to an ecumenical (Presbyterian, Lutheran, and Catholic) gathering of laity and clergy. This resulted in dreaming about doing a community-based youth ministry and possibly jointly hiring a youth worker.

At one of these meetings, there was real interest and excitement about doing a community survey. After the meeting, the participants began second-guessing the process. "Maybe we could just do a mail survey instead of going door to door." The process faded away before anything got started. At another gathering, one of the pastors offered to convene an ecumenical youth task force, but there was no follow-up. The energy around these ideas dissipated, so nothing more happened.

During the fall 2000 professional interview,[6] the pastor confided in me that he thought that if he were out of the picture, the congregation would feel freer to proceed with definite steps. Part of the conversation I had had with the parish was that they no longer were statistically a full-time appointment (our guideline is that one full-time staff person is needed for each 100 in average worship attendance). His observation was confirmed by the fact that it was becoming increasingly difficult for the Miles congregation to meet its financial obligations. The trends were as follows:

Ten-Year Statistical Information for Miles UMC

	1991	1992	1993	1994	1995	1996	1997	1998	1999	2000
Membership	43	43	41	40	36	36	35	33	32	32
Worship attendance	NA	13	14	17	17	17	18	15	12	10
Confirmation of faith	1	1	1	0	0	0	0	0	0	0
Baptisms	3	3	0	0	0	0	0	0	0	0

I met with the staff-pastor parish relationship committee on January 30, 2001, and at that meeting the pastor announced his intention to be considered for a move in June. The pastor was beloved, so it was difficult for the people to hear, but they did understand his reasons (his desire to allow the churches to reconfigure their staffing and his wish to be closer to grandchildren). This disclosure prompted two matters for consideration:

1. A request to consider decreasing the pastoral appointment from full- to three-quarter time. A charge conference was set for February 15, 2001, to do this, effective July 1, 2001.
2. A more serious inquiry regarding specific steps for closing Miles Church.

A new pastor was appointed to the parish on a three-quarter-time basis. He indicated that he welcomed a "challenge." I encouraged the folks at Miles to take advantage of this new energy to see what would happen. Although an honest effort was made to "try again," the enthusiasm of the new pastor was not sufficient to turn the tide. I was asked to schedule a charge conference on September 20, 2001, to close Miles Church.

Miles Church had the only parsonage available for use in the parish, and the congregation offered to transfer title of the parsonage to the other two churches in the parish. The offer was accepted, so the church facility was put up for bids. The first round of bidding did not solicit any bidders. Eventually, private negotiations did result in the sale of the church building to a local contractor.

The concluding worship was scheduled for October 7, 2001. The entire parish was invited to a joint service of worship. Extended family members and former parishioners were invited back for the occasion. About 200 people attended the celebration, concluding 125 years of faithful ministry through this congregation. Many of the members had already begun plans to relate to nearby congregations, in most cases one of the two remaining congregations in the parish, and the pastor of the parish will process the transfer of membership upon request.

Conclusion

Many people think of the church as their anchor in the midst of rapid change and shifting values. All three of these congregations had been around well beyond a century and had a history in their community. These churches had been a holy place for generations of families. Every time a business or institution ceases to exist in a rural community, these strong descendants of pioneers face change that may have a dramatic effect on their way of life. Still, rural folks are stewards of the earth, so they understand life cycles. Thinking about a business or church having a life cycle helps them to understand the closing, but their response to that closing, especially the closing of a church, is not the same as what they feel when harvesting a stalk of wheat or sending a yearling steer to market.

Pastors and denominational representatives who care for the members of these rural congregations need to keep in mind the significant level of struggle and pain felt by those involved in closing a church. The message they need to communicate is simple: The fact that a worshiping congregation will no longer meet at the usual spot does not change the fact that each individual is a beloved child of God, and it is this assurance that makes it possible to conclude the life of a church with hope.

NOTES

1. A charge conference is the authorized body that makes substantive decisions for a congregation. It is the body that does the annual business of electing officers, setting budgets, giving direction for ministry, and so forth. The membership of a charge conference is the administrative board or council. This conference may also be convened as a church conference in which the entire congregation participates as voting members.

2. "Procedure for Closing a Church," as provided in the 2000 United Methodist Church Book of Discipline.

3. Trust Clause, 2000 United Methodist Church Book of Discipline, paragraph 2501–3, is a covenant in which the local church has full responsibility for the property. The Trust Clause imposes restrictions that prohibit change in the use or disposition of the facility from its original intent unless a majority of the local congregation and the designated annual conference representatives concur.

4. I have had conversations about this factor in numerous places. In my first appointment in a three-point parish, people were also adamant about needing to keep small churches open because "people won't travel further." Every week

these same dear folks got into their cars after worship and drove 30 miles for lunch in the opposite direction from where they lived.

5. Bi-district Conference Council on Ministry program staff member, one of six staff deployed in the annual conference to resource local churches.

6. Iowa district superintendents schedule annual formal interviews with all clergy under appointment to provide support, establish spiritual accountability ("How is it with your soul?"), dialogue to aid in supervision, and discuss any anticipated/desired changes in appointment for the next year.

10

A Struggle to the End

Cynthia Marie Chapa

It is a Monday evening in the late fall of 1999, and approximately 12 men and women, long-time members of Bethlehem Lutheran Church in Houston, Texas, are gathered around a table for the regular bimonthly voters' meeting. They convene in the same parish hall where the ladies guild holds its still popular hamburger fry on the third Thursday of each month (a tradition of over 50 years), where the annual men's club mission festival barbecue has been served year after year, and where senior citizens join monthly for a game of bingo. It is not the first time that the voting members of this church have broached the odious question, Is it time to close our doors?

Bethlehem had never been large in numbers. In its glory days it had boasted perhaps 350 to 400 adult members and a Sunday school enrollment of 280. Reflecting its modest membership, the church's facilities were anything but opulent. The simple sanctuary could hold a maximum of 200 people. The parish hall building with its two classrooms, ample kitchen space, and restrooms was adequate for the 100 to 150 guests who appeared at various meals, festivals, and functions.

Nor did the congregation of Bethlehem have a particularly long or illustrious tradition. Its history reached back only 60-some years to the World War II era, when a small group split off from nearby Trinity Lutheran Church in downtown Houston to establish a congregation in which German would continue to be the language of worship. Most of Bethlehem's early members had migrated approximately 100 miles from the rural areas around Giddings, LaGrange, and Serbin, Texas. These were farming communities that had been settled by German immigrants in the late 1800s. Economic pressures around the time of the depression prompted the children and grandchildren of these farmers to move to Houston in search of employment and a better standard of living. Yet their language at home and particularly their language of worship remained German. Consequently, Bethlehem's founding fathers drafted a charter and constitution that stipulated the use of German as well as English in public services "so long as one communicant member of the congregation insisted upon it." The first worship services took place in October 1940 and were held in a local elementary school. By April 1941, the small group had secured its first called pastor, the Reverend Anton Froehlich.

Under Pastor Froehlich's leadership, the congregation grew in size and energy. Land was purchased at the corner of 12th and Studewood Streets in the heart of the "Heights" area of Houston. One of the city's oldest neighborhoods, the Heights borders on downtown. At the time of Bethlehem's formation, it was a quiet, residential neighborhood populated primarily by working-class whites. Their modest but tidy homes were generally one-story, wood-frame structures. Tree-lined streets, well-kept yards, friendly local merchants, community parks and activities all contributed to the tranquility, security, and congeniality of the area.

Having secured property, Bethlehem members moved quickly to construct a place of worship. Ground was broken on July 13, 1941, and the completed brick structure was dedicated on December 14 of the same year. Less than three years later, a Christian day school offering grades 1 through 6 was established. The congregation flourished and activities abounded as children and grandchildren born to the first generation of members were baptized, schooled, and confirmed there. Eventually the school was expanded to include kindergarten through grade eight. Three church services were conducted each Sunday, two in English and one in German. The day school, men's club, ladies guild, and youth league ensured continuous activities throughout the week, in the evenings, and on Sundays. The vitality of the congregation was evidenced in the fact that three of its "sons" entered into full-time ministry.

Bethlehem congregation was able to sustain a vibrant church life in this manner for nearly 30 years. Its families were strong, devout, hard working, and dedicated to Bethlehem's continuance. New members were regularly added, primarily through marriage or transfer from other Lutheran churches. Some of these newcomers found the smallness and family-like character of the church appealing. Others were attracted by the perpetuation of the German tradition, although the German service was discontinued in 1972 after the retirement of the church's second pastor, Henry Traugott. The school was also a significant drawing card for new members. Yet, once the children and grandchildren of the original congregation had completed their nine years of schooling at Bethlehem, it became difficult for the church to maintain its robustness.

A gradual downturn in membership began in the early 1970s, due in large part to the changing demographics of the neighborhood surrounding the church. When Bethlehem was established, most of its members lived in the immediate Heights neighborhood. It was in every sense a local church, just a few minutes by car from the homes of its members. Then, in the '60s and '70s a migration of Houston's urban population into the suburbs took place. Many of the middle-class homeowners in the Heights sold their modest frame houses and purchased large, modern, brick dwellings five, 15, or even 20 miles away. Some of the older Bethlehem members remained in the area, but many of them and virtually all of their children succumbed to the lure of suburbia. Though a number of those who moved away remained loyal members, their ability to be actively involved in congregational life was greatly curtailed by the longer commute. Typically, they sent their own children to nearby public schools rather than transporting them to Bethlehem School in the Heights. With diminishing church membership, financial resources, and student enrollment, the task of maintaining a full-scale school became a daunting challenge.

Not more than a mile away from Bethlehem was a larger and older congregation, Immanuel Lutheran. It too had a grade school. In the late 1960s, as Bethlehem found it increasingly difficult to support a school on its own, leaders from both congregations agreed to join forces and create Immanuel-Bethlehem Lutheran School. Preschool through first grade classes were held on the Bethlehem campus, grades 2 through 8 on the Immanuel campus. This arrangement prevailed for more than 25 years, giving the smaller congregation, always in a state of slow but steady decline, a reason to exist.

Throughout these years of gradual weakening, Bethlehem congregation and its various pastors were keenly aware that there must be an outreach into the neighborhood in order to bring the gospel to the unchurched and perhaps gain new members. The properties in the Heights that had been vacated in favor of suburbia were for the most part rented by low-income Hispanics, many of them newly immigrated from Central and South America. Motivated by Christ's Great Commission, Bethlehem organized several efforts to evangelize in this new and foreign community. The consistent futility of these endeavors finally moved the congregation in 1994 to call a

Spanish-speaking Anglo pastor. In a well-intentioned but awkward attempt to surmount the language and culture barriers, this pastor added more contemporary ingredients to the worship experience at Bethlehem, playing his guitar to accompany nontraditional hymns and introducing a Spanish song or two. He initiated separate Spanish services on Sunday evenings for a six-month trial period and made door-to-door visits to drum up interest. It was all to no avail. The Hispanics were unmoved. At most they would send their children to vacation Bible school each summer, but follow-up visits to their homes yielded no results at Sunday worship.

Understandably, these Latinos were not inclined to seek a church home in an English-speaking congregation and in an atmosphere where not only the language but also the Protestant traditions were foreign to them. Catholic churches, to which they could more easily relate, were available in the area and in most cases had instituted Spanish services. Added to this, however, was the lackluster quality of Bethlehem's outreach. Although intellectually convinced that the gospel is to be preached "to all nations," some of the leading members were less than warm to the prospect of taking in foreign elements that might disrupt their church's identity and beloved traditions. As a result, there was little "fire" in attempts to evangelize among Hispanics.

In the meantime, the Heights neighborhood was again undergoing a radical transformation. Beginning in the early 1980s there was an explosion of interest in the old vintage homes in the area. Many were purchased and restored in their original style. Parks and esplanades were beautified. Massive new construction of fashionable Victorian-style houses and condos transfigured once shabby streets. Consequently, properties soared in value, many Hispanics were forced to move out, and the area became a mecca for upscale professionals. Once again, Bethlehem organized door-to-door evangelism visits, but this new pool of prospective members also proved an unproductive mission field. By this time the congregation was too small and unexciting to attract the trendy crowd. Bethlehem's future seemed less hopeful than ever.

Perhaps the crowning blow in this downward development was the decision by Immanuel in 1996 to discontinue the school partnership with Bethlehem. The larger congregation hoped to eliminate administrative difficulties and strengthen its ministry by concentrating the whole range of classes from prekindergarten through eighth grade on its own campus. This decision brought to a head Bethlehem's long years of soul searching. The congregation was literally dying out as old members passed on, younger ones transferred out in search of a more vibrant church fellowship, and few if any new members were gained. To add to the congregation's difficulties, the young pastor who had served there since 1994 returned to seminary in 1998 for advanced studies, leaving the beleaguered parishioners once more without a leader.

Throughout the course of these changes, there remained a core group of lay members who were passionately committed to the church and willing to seek new avenues of growth. In about 1995, for example, the congregation called in a representative from the Texas District to do a demographic study of the neighborhood and provide a seminar on how the congregation might get back on its feet. Ideas were exchanged, and possible new ministries appropriate to the area were discussed. A Mother's Day Out program and a senior citizens' center came under consideration. Start-up resources had been saved for such a program, so that finances were never really an issue. Yet it was difficult for the small group to reach consensus on what precisely to do, and most importantly, no one had the courage or the know-how to step forward, commit to a program, and then follow through. It was overwhelming to think that this handful of people, in which only two couples were younger than 50, would have to start this effort from scratch and then find a way to sustain it.

An excellent, spirit-filled, visionary pastor might have led the congregation into new territory for growth. Yet how could a languishing congregation of this size attract such a person? Where was that self-sacrificing leader with vision, determination, expertise, and charisma? This "super pastor" would also have to possess extraordinary leadership and diplomacy skills in order to handle the resistance to change among those members entrenched in "the Bethlehem way of doing things." For over 20 years, Anton Froehlich had been successful in steering the resolute and at times obstinate Germans under his leadership. After his death in 1962, a succession of six pastors served the church, each with varying degrees of influence but none with the ability to reverse the trend toward decline. Over the final 10 years of its existence, as the church lost its pastors through call to other congregations, retirement, or change in career plans, the lay members were faced repeatedly with the haunting dilemma of whether to fold or to try once more.

This was again the question at hand as the voters convened on this fall evening in 1999. For over a year, since the last pastor's resignation, the church had been served by visiting preachers who appeared only on

Sunday mornings. This hiatus in leadership only exacerbated the weakening process and made closing seem virtually inevitable. And yet the option to close was not the only item on the agenda that evening. As recently as the spring of 1999, an unexpected though dim glimmer of hope for continued ministry at Bethlehem had arisen. A burgeoning congregation some 10 miles away in the Spring Branch area of Houston was considering establishing a satellite church in the Heights. If Bethlehem was interested, the larger church was prepared to entertain the idea of seeding the congregation with perhaps 80 of its own members, holding evangelistic training sessions, and then undertaking vigorous outreach programs in the area. Although to some Bethlehem members this was an overture that offered hope of revival, others were wary of the proposal. They feared that Bethlehem would lose its identity in the process and that unfamiliar contemporary worship styles would be introduced in an effort to increase attendance. There was still a small but vocal contingent set on retaining the church's name, its cherished traditions, and its self-determination.

Consequently, rather than accept this offer, the congregation voted to make one last effort to resurrect itself. At this point, the average Sunday attendance was down to about 25, not enough to warrant calling a new pastor. Instead, an interim pastor who was retired and had filled in several times during the long vacancy was hired under contract for an indefinite period of time. Perhaps, it was thought, the remaining members together with this pastor could "dig in"; that is, try hard and ultimately revive the congregation. If attendance increased, a pastor would be called.

A year passed, but numbers did not increase. Although the ladiesguild hamburger fry continued to be well attended and the senior citizens' bingo remained popular, Bethlehem failed to attract new members. Young people and couples with children were most conspicuously absent. As one means of bolstering the congregation, the interim pastor suggested that a homecoming festival and barbecue be organized in October 2000, the church's 60th anniversary. Over 100 people came, some from long distances, to fill the church's pews and to celebrate its warm history. But this was not a pool for new members. No one from the neighborhood who was not already a member appeared. The occasion, though happy and festive, turned out to be a farewell to bygone days.

Nevertheless, an alternative to the closing of the church had presented itself almost miraculously in June 2000. A former member of Bethlehem, now an elder at Immanuel, had asked in casual conversation at the monthly hamburger fry if there would be any interest in Bethlehem's working together with Immanuel. The latter congregation was entering into a massive and ambitious church growth program. Physical expansion was limited due to the church's landlocked location in a residential neighborhood. Bethlehem's assets, in particular its property, might be helpful in this effort.

By now the few remaining Bethlehemites were open to the suggestion of joining forces with a larger congregation. The two churches had a history of cooperation, albeit disjointed and at times disappointing to the smaller church. A partnership with Immanuel was at least more appealing than the total extinction of Bethlehem. Various meetings involving leaders from both congregations took place between June and November 2000. As discussions began to center on the idea of merger, a representative from the Texas District was invited to give pertinent information on the legalities, implications, and processes attendant upon this option. Essentially, merger would mean dissolving Bethlehem and the turning over of all assets to Immanuel. The only other model for merger would require that both congregations dissolve and an entirely new congregation apply for a charter with the State of Texas. The latter option would have involved Immanuel in untold legal, administrative, and organizational entanglements. It was never given serious consideration.

When on December 11, 2000, Bethlehem voters met to vote on a merger, older members in particular were heavy of heart. They recoiled from the prospect of finishing out their days in any other church. This, after all, was their beloved place of worship and Christian service. Clearly, if the merger was approved, there was little hope of continued regular Sunday morning services at Bethlehem. This was the cruelest blow for the older folk. At this late stage they would have to choose a new home church, and the effort required for such a transition seemed almost unbearable. Yet even the most diehard members had to admit that this was probably the only viable option. As one dear lady put it, "There are so few of us here on Sunday morning that it's hard for us to even produce the Lord's Prayer audibly, and our hymn singing is pathetic." It was true. Although the church had once boasted two fine organists and a good choir, there was no longer a talented musician left to accompany the meager Sunday morning singing.

Those less deeply rooted in the Bethlehem tradition were more willing not only to entertain, but even to welcome the thought of merger. It was at least a chance to see ministry continue on this campus—this piece of property so well situated on the corner of a much-traveled main street in the Heights. Bethlehem members who transferred to Immanuel would have a voice in determining how best to use the facilities. There had already been discussion at Immanuel of perhaps using the small sanctuary for an occasional youth group contemporary service. The ample grounds were ideal for recreation and picnicking. The parish hall could be used immediately for meetings, Bible studies, funeral luncheons, and receptions. Perhaps in the future an early childhood education program or a senior citizens' activity center could be established here. Both churches were in agreement that the hamburger fry and the bingo should be retained on what would be called the Bethlehem Campus of Immanuel Lutheran Church.

Thus, at this pivotal meeting in December 2000, the Bethlehem group voted reluctantly but unanimously for merger with Immanuel. In January 2001, Immanuel members agreed to the merger as well.

Meanwhile, Bethlehem's interim pastor had received another employment offer and announced that he would only be able to serve the church through March 2001. This led to the decision that the final morning worship service at Bethlehem Lutheran Church would be held on the last Sunday in March. A formal decommissioning service could be held at a future date.

The December 11 decision was communicated by one of the Bethlehem members to the Texas District. Clear instructions were given by that office concerning the steps to follow in planning a decommissioning service, dispersing assets, turning over all remaining real and financial holdings to Immanuel, and finally filing with the State of Texas for legal dissolution. Bethlehem voters continued to meet on a regular basis to decide how best to use their considerable financial resources. Two educational endowment funds with the Bethlehem name were established, one at Houston's Lutheran High School Association and one at Concordia College in Austin. Generous lump sums were donated to favorite charities: Lutheran Church—Missouri Synod World Missions, Houston Lutherans for Life, Houston's new intercultural LINC (Lutheran Intercity Network Coalition) ministry, and the Houston Area Lutheran Council. Finally, large amounts were donated to Immanuel's "Reaching for His Heights" evangelism program as well as to its general fund.

Meanwhile, a Texas District representative in the area was consulted for guidance on how to design a service of decommissioning. The program was planned by a few of the remaining Bethlehem members and was held on the afternoon of April 29, 2001. Four pastors officiated: the recent interim pastor, one of the church's former pastors, Immanuel's pastor, and the lead pastor in Bethlehem's circuit. The occasion was celebratory in nature, centering on the great God who had established this congregation, the way God had blessed it through the years and now, the new direction its members were being given by God. At the conclusion of the service, the circuit counselor officially decommissioned the congregation and then recommissioned the members of Bethlehem to the Lord's work in other congregations. Following the formal portion of the service, several current and former members were given the opportunity to reminisce publicly about their personal Bethlehem experience. Once again the church was filled to overflowing as in its heyday. Informal reminiscing continued in the parish hall over refreshments served by the ladies guild following the church service. Understandably, tears and sighs abounded, but a general feeling of calm acceptance prevailed.

Of the 20 members or so who faithfully attended Bethlehem to the end, more than half transferred to Immanuel. The transition was smooth, owing in large part to the way the two congregations had been connected through the years. Immanuel members extended themselves in a genuinely warm, welcoming, and nurturing manner. Within weeks the former Bethlehemites were reveling in the benefits of a vigorous and many-faceted congregational life. Those who did not join Immanuel sought out other Lutheran churches in their neighborhoods, some relieved at last to be able to bid adieu to Bethlehem with a clear conscience.

Undoubtedly, each Bethlehem member would have his or her own story to tell of the joys and sorrows at this church and the wrenching decision to close it. Yet time has passed, and the pain of that decision has subsided. To all appearances, the church at Bethlehem has successfully dispersed its children into the comforting arms of the larger Lutheran family, and with that, into the Lord's invisible church universal.

11

Ending with Strength

Lowell L. Hesterman

When compared with the stories of many congregational closings, that of Lutheran Church of the Master in Edina, Minnesota, is unusual. The decision to disband was made when worship attendance was still about average for a Protestant church in the United States, and the church building sat on a valuable piece of real estate. The trends for key indicators of congregational health were all downward, however, and members made a powerful choice: to close before they had nothing left to share with the wider church and community.

The Beginning Period (1959–1961)

In 1959, the Evangelical Lutheran Church (ELC) established a new congregation in Edina, Minnesota. "A four-acre site was purchased at France Avenue South and 72nd Street, situated in an area surrounded by sand dunes and gravel pits. It seemed an unlikely place for a new church, but the success of the new Southdale Shopping Center indicated that more and more people would move into the area."[1] The site was located just two blocks south of Southdale, the first major enclosed mall in America. The highly visible site provided ample parking space for immediate and future needs.

The first worship service for Lutheran Church of the Master (LCM) was held on June 7, 1959. The organizing pastor, assisted by a parish worker salaried by the ELC, arranged for services in the auditorium of a large department store in Southdale. Forty-six families, including 82 confirmed and 164 baptized members, were listed when the charter was closed in November. We assume that one-half of the charter members were children under 14. When the congregation held its final service on March 9, 1997, there were fewer than 10 children under 18 years of age.

Edina, one of the most affluent suburbs in the Minneapolis area, boasted a school system rated among the best in the Twin Cities. The neighborhood was still being developed with expensive single-family homes. Many residents were young, professional families with preschool and elementary-age children. Because Lutherans are the most numerous among Protestants in Minnesota, it could be assumed that many of Edina's residents were Lutherans. By some criteria, the site for the new church seemed perfect.

In retrospect, there were disadvantages. Southdale Mall stretched from France Avenue on the west to York Avenue on the east. The west side of France, where LCM was situated, became almost exclusively commercial. The area immediately east of LCM, nearly a square mile in size, became commercial, except for some senior apartments and condominiums. Residents east of York Avenue were as near, or nearer, to another ELC congregation. Also, in 1959, a sister Lutheran denomination started a new mission, St. Stephen, a mile and a half south of LCM.

Period of Growth (1961–1969)

The second pastor arrived in 1961 to succeed Pastor Smith, and under his leadership the congregation experienced rapid growth during the 1960s, growth reflected in its building programs.

The first worship unit, with a seating capacity of 175, was dedicated in 1959. An educational unit was started in July 1961 to accommodate the overflowing Sunday school. On November 5, 1967, only eight years after its founding, ground was broken for an office wing and a new sanctuary with seating for 425.

The baptized membership increased rapidly from 164 at the end of 1959 to its all-time peak of 725 ten years later. Interestingly, Sunday school enrollment reached a peak of 359[2] in 1965, four years before the congregation as a whole peaked, but decreased to 317 by the end of 1969.

The Period of Plateau and Decline (1970–1991)

During the next two decades, LCM continued as a healthy congregation. Although the baptized membership dipped below 700 in 1971 and below 600 in 1977, the confirmed membership experienced a loss of only 12 during this period. Baby boomers were moving from childhood, through high school, to college age and then disappearing, not to be replaced with a new crop of young children.

Financially, the congregation remained vigorous. It assumed a $200,000 building program in 1967 without difficulty and demonstrated its outward vision of the church's mission the same year by committing to a missionary sponsorship program, raising annually over the next 18 years between $7,500 and $15,000 for this extra-mile program. In 1975, its members donated $112,000 for a special American Lutheran Church (ALC) United Mission Appeal.

After the departure of the parish worker who had helped establish LCM, the congregation moved to staffing structures that included a secretary, a series of seminary students, or assistant pastors who served as part-time youth workers. In 1984, Bruce Kuenzel joined Pastor Williams in a team ministry. One year later, the senior pastor retired. James Lindekugel joined the staff in September 1985 as the senior pastor.

A hint of financial difficulty arose in 1987 when the council felt the congregation could not support two full-time pastors and, with reluctance, advised Pastor Kuenzel to make himself available for call. With Pastor Kuenzel's departure, the congregation reverted to a succession of part-time youth workers in the belief that "the youth are the future of the congregation."

This assessment was partly correct. Without a good youth program, member families with youngsters might transfer to other congregations, and new families might be reluctant to join. But hiring a youth worker did not result in retaining or attracting youth. Few high school graduates remained in the congregation. Job markets and the high housing costs were obstacles to their remaining in the community.

By 1985, Sunday school enrollment in this maturing congregation had dropped to 112. The average church attendance decreased from 285 in 1986 to 170 in 1993.

Events in 1987 may have moved the congregation to the brink of vulnerability. A misunderstanding between the pastor and the president of the congregation led the president to resign and transfer to another church. Concurrently, 12 leadership families and four couples, for a variety of reasons, transferred to other congregations. They were Sunday school teachers, committee leaders, and generous contributors. Their departure produced a domino effect, decreasing the size of Sunday school classes and youth groups, thereby making the congregation less attractive to visitors.

Former members of LCM now look back upon 1989 and 1990 as "What if?" years. A program/facilities task force, concluding that the 30- and 20-year-old sections of the building would require $200,000 in repairs, brought to the congregation four alternatives: (1) maintain and remodel existing facilities; (2) relocate and rebuild; (3) sell an acre of property and rebuild; (4) do nothing. The task force prepared a questionnaire for the congregation about these options.

Only 57 questionnaires were returned from 240 families, a disquietingly low number. Alternative 3 received 28 votes, hardly a mandate. The task force had reasoned that if the congregation applied the cost of anticipated repairs, used the proceeds from the sale of the parsonage, and accepted a $1,000,000 offer it had received for the purchase of 1.18 acres of its land, the congregation would have a good start toward the cost of a new building. With hesitation, it recommended alternative 3 to the council.

The task force's report included these statements. "If we assumed our baptized membership would grow to 640 in five years and 700 in 10 years with an average attendance of 48 percent, . . . we would have an average attendance of 336 for two services, thus a seating capacity of 280 does allow for future growth."[3] Later in the report, however, this caution was included: "Our Task Force has a major concern that if we undertake a building program and we do not grow in membership we will be in serious financial difficulty. However the alternative appears to be a continuing decline."[4]

What if the congregation had followed the recommendation of the task force? Would a new and more appropriately designed building have changed LCM's future?

The possible sale planted a seed in the minds of a few members. If one acre of this prime site could be sold for a million dollars, would the sale of all four acres bring between three and four million dollars? If so, wouldn't it be better stewardship to sell the property and use the proceeds for mission? Even though the estimated value proved to be incorrect, a seed was sown.

Simultaneously, the congregation explored possible consolidation with other neighboring Lutheran congregations. Conversations resulted in the formation of a combined confirmation class. When LCM declared that two givens were that LCM's location had to be used and its pastor called to serve the combined congregation, however, the merger felt more like a takeover to one of the congregations, and the proposed consolidation failed.

The church council, seeking a solution to declining membership, sought advice from church planners every year between 1987 to 1995 to try to develop new goals, visions, and ministries. The congregation also reached out to the community by opening its doors to meals-on-wheels, a nursery school, the Midwest Gluten Intolerance Group, Alcoholics Anonymous and, in 1996, a 250-member Russian immigrant congregation.

Plateau and Decline Period Membership Statistics

Year	Baptized	Confirmed	Average Attend.	S.S.
1969	725	442	?	317
1979	541	431	264	179
1989	562	478	199	62
1992	428	374	191	17

Although the baptized membership had declined by nearly 300 between 1969 and 1992, the confirmed membership declined only by 68. The Sunday school enrollment shows that the age pyramid became inverted, and seniors became the dominant group.

The Period of Escalating Decline (1991–1996)

The decreased attendance took its toll on church finances. In 1991, the budget committee, faced with rising fixed costs while the total income was decreasing, recommended a two-thirds decrease in benevolences (offerings from the congregation to the judicatory and national expressions of the church). More bad news followed. Between 1986 and 1993, the salary, allowances, and custodial budget lines had increased by $38,369 while the total budget had decreased by $25,162. Rally day attendance dipped to 24 in 1993. Children's sermons were eliminated. In 1994, only three new members were received, while 27 members transferred away. Church attendance dropped from 191 in 1992 to under 100 in March 1995.

A pivotal moment developed during budget preparations for 1996. It became obvious, after $15,000 reductions in income in each of the previous three years, that minor reductions in expenditures would not suffice. The only option to attain a balanced budget would be to reduce staff. To drop the leaders of the excellent music program could be counterproductive. To reduce the pastor's position to part-time would simply hasten the downward spiral. One member read a statement, "The Pain of Downsizing." Another member, quoting from John 12:24, said, "Perhaps, like a grain of wheat, we need to die so that there can be more fruit." For the first time, dissolving the congregation became a serious option. The president concluded, "We had come to a crossroad," and he urged that a congregation meeting should be called to consider the future.

First, however, a meeting was scheduled with the synod bishop, David Olson, who outlined three options: (1) continue as we are; (2) die and rebuild (form a new congregation with a new style of ministry); (3) give up our life for the sake of new life. In effect, the bishop gave the congregation permission to consider closing.

In his report to the January 28, 1996, special congregational meeting, the president of the congregation referred to a $35,566 decrease in anticipated income and also announced that a developer had made a firm offer to buy the property. He presented a series of recommendations from the council, including the scheduling of three meetings on February 5, 1996, to give all members a chance to voice their concerns, hopes, and recommendations.

At these meetings, several council members provided charts that showed the downward trends in all the numerical measures of the congregation's life. The members were asked to reflect on these reports and to voice their views at four separate home meetings scheduled for April 14, 15, 16, and 17.

The three options discussed at these well-attended home meetings were those outlined by Bishop Olson. The core members, who had a deep love and concern for the congregation as a whole and for members individually, engaged in lively discussions. Some expressed hope, some vowed to fight on, but many concluded that it was better to close while there was still strength, rather than to die slowly in an atmosphere of despair and frustration. It is not surprising that some members criticized the pastor who served during this period of decline. A few criticized the synod for not doing more to help, but no one could define what that help might be. A frequently voiced thought was, "Let's not prolong this indefinitely. Perhaps we've bottomed out, but if not, let's come to closure soon."

Closure (1996–1998)

During the next few months, the congregation council decided to call a special congregation meeting for Sunday, July 28, to act on several resolutions, two of which were key: "To authorize the council to negotiate a Development Agreement and a Purchase Agreement with one of the developers submitting proposals . . ." and "To authorize the council to hire legal counsel to assist in negotiating agreements described in resolution 1." Realizing that these actions could be the first steps toward dissolution, members engaged in thoughtful and spirited discussion. The resolutions passed by a vote of 71 to 54.

At the meeting, some said that they could not vote for closure unless they knew how the assets would be dispersed. A team was formed to prepare a recommendation for the distribution of the financial assets in such a way that the witness and ministry of LCM would continue. Members were invited to present written recommendations, as were the Evangelical Lutheran Church in America's (ELCA) Division for Global Mission, the ELCA's Mission Founders, the synod bishop, Luther Seminary in St. Paul, and Volunteers Enlisted to Assist People (VEAP), a local ecumenical organization to assist people with food and financial needs.

The team developed four categories of gifts: global mission, new congregation starts in the United States (Mission Founders), synod projects, and other church-related ministries, including Christian education and community service projects. (The third and fourth categories were later combined.) Although an estimated $1,450,000 could be allocated, the committee received requests totaling $4,836,900. It then appointed a subcommittee to devise several "packages" that could be funded—with an approximate balance in the three categories.

In a report to the congregation dated October 30, 1996, the secretary summarized the principles, although unwritten, that guided the subcommittee. Consideration would be given to:

1. agencies/ministries to which members had previously contributed
2. ministries supported by virtue of LCM's constitution
3. ministries that would be anticipating an annual gift from the congregation's Lenten offerings, and the missionary sponsorship program
4. the long-term effects of the gifts
5. the establishment of new congregations, because the congregation had received assistance from the ELC when it was formed

At the advice of the attorney, the subcommittee also decided funds should be directed only to ministries of the Lutheran church.

Although several adjustments had to be made when the final accounting was completed, the congregation approved these recommendations:[5]

The Evangelical Lutheran Church in America, for an endowed mission position[5a]	$ 500,000
Mission Founders, for two new congregations	300,000
Luther Seminary, for the Fredrik Schiotz Chair of Christian Mission[5b]	295,000
Jordan New Life Lutheran Church, north Minneapolis, an inner-city mission	57,500
Calvary Lutheran, south Minneapolis, for inner-city programs	55,000
Holy Cross Lutheran Church, Rockport, Texas	10,000
St. Stephen Lutheran Church	2,500
Mission Builders	40,000
Mount Carmel Ministries[5c]	30,000
Global Health Ministries	12,000
VEAP	20,000
Eight gifts of $1,000 to eight charities	8,000
	$1,330,000

This report was instrumental in helping members visualize the mission that could be accomplished if the congregation dissolved and distributed its assets.

Following the July meeting, the council entered into negotiations with the developer who had offered $1,450,000 to purchase the property to build a three-story office building. A special meeting of the congregation was called for February 9, 1997, to vote on the three resolutions drawn up by the attorney. By a solid 73 to 10 vote, resolutions were approved to suspend the activities of the congregation on March 9, 1997, to adopt the plan for the distribution of the church's assets, and to dissolve Lutheran Church of the Master.

Several factors helped to ease the pain of this decision. As a result of the 1988 merger of Lutheran denominations, there were now 19 ELCA congregations within a four-mile radius of LCM. If LCM closed, no member would be more than two miles from an ELCA congregation. Those members who used the LCM van lived in condominiums and apartments also served by transportation from other Lutheran churches. From a stewardship point, these members could be reached in a more cost-effective manner from these neighboring congregations.

Perhaps even more importantly, the members began to realize that closing did not mean defeat. The congregation could celebrate the fact that it had provided Word and Sacrament ministry for 38 years, its youth were providing leadership for congregations elsewhere, and it had supported the church's broader work in a meaningful and generous way.

Because the developer would demolish the building, arrangements were made to dispose of all movable property and equipment. Members were given the first opportunity to purchase items. Furnishings and equipment, including the organ, bells, the large outdoor symbols, the large cross that had hung in the first sanctuary, and even the outdoor lamps leading to the sanctuary entrance were given or sold to other congregations or church institutions. Tables, desks, dishes, ovens, paraments, and communion ware were put to use elsewhere. A mission congregation removed the oak molding from the fellowship hall for its building program, while a Bible camp removed all the electrical outlets and fixtures to use in its construction program. Even the bathroom fixtures were removed. After the last service, members were invited to take a hymnal home as a keepsake.

After the decision had been made to close, much hard work remained. At the suggestion of its attorney, the congregation authorized the council to continue to serve as a "legal body" to complete the sale of the property, provide termination benefits for the staff, help members relocate, pay remaining bills, provide insurance coverage, deposit important documents with the archives at Luther Seminary and a neighboring congregation, and so forth.

The property sale encountered a snag when a neighborhood group protested the proposed plans, and negotiations with a new developer had to begin. The council president and the attorney worked tirelessly to develop a win-win solution for the community, the congregation, and the developer. A second developer secured the necessary rezoning permit to build an assisted living complex, a beautiful facility that solved many of the issues the neighborhood raised while providing a needed service to the community.

Although March 2, 1997, had been set for presenting checks to the selected recipients, the unexpected delay meant that these gifts could not be distributed; however, several recipients were present at a special worship service to thank the congregation. The Reverend Bonnie Jensen, speaking for the Division for Global Mission, said, "What is so meaningful to me is that this is a personal sacrifice, much like our missionaries make. Members of this congregation are denying themselves in order to give this gift to the mission of Christ." Members began to visualize the seeds for mission that were being sown.

The final service the following Sunday was much more solemn. After the congregation's final participation in the Lord's Supper and benediction, the pulpit and altar furnishings were removed. There were tears and hugs, grief and sadness. A sense of mission was expressed by Pastor Lindekugel: "All that God is asking is to give up our fellowship. Was the building our church? No, we are the church."

During the summer, the council members telephoned each family to ask if they had joined another congregation and to encourage them if they had not. Neighboring ELCA congregations had been kept informed of LCM's developments. Special visits had been arranged at two of the churches to help members become acquainted with membership opportunities. As former members transferred to other congregations, they were quickly assimilated and even welcomed into leadership roles. There were numerous anecdotal comments to the effect that "it's good to belong to a congregation that is actively engaged in mission, where there is a positive attitude, a variety of programs, and a joy in worship."

When the sale was finally completed and all outstanding bills paid, plans could be made for a service on May 3, 1998, for the distribution of the congregation's financial assets. St. Stephen offered to host this service. A planning committee began preparations. Because there were no liturgies available for services held after a church had closed, the committee developed its own liturgy with the theme "Sowing Seeds for Mission."[6] With stalks of wheat at his side, the Reverend Gil Helgesen, a member of LCM's congregation council, based his sermon on John 12:24. Then came the long-awaited thrill of giving the gifts according to these groupings:

Sowing Seeds for Mission through Acts of Love
Sowing Seeds for Mission through New Ministries
Sowing Seeds for Mission through Christian Nurture
Sowing Seeds for Mission throughout the World

An appropriate hymn, scripture reading, and prayer introduced each grouping. Members then escorted the recipients to the chancel, read from a prepared script, and joyfully distributed checks totaling $1,330,000 as seeds for mission. *Soli Deo Gloria*.

The long delay proved beneficial. It allowed time for mourning and healing. After the service, as the former members gathered in St. Stephen's Activity Center, a family-reunion-like atmosphere pervaded the room as former members greeted one another with smiles, hugs, and joyful sharing of stories about their new church homes.

Epilogue

Even though the congregation dissolved, remnants continue. A women's circle continues to meet regularly as does a men's Wednesday morning breakfast group. A golf team continues. Notices of funerals of former members spread quickly, and members gather to recognize their former colleagues. Fruits of the congregation's seeds for mission were observed when 70 former members gathered in August 2001 to hear reports from the missionaries LCM's gifts had sponsored. New congregations have arisen because Lutheran Church of the Master chose to give up its life so that new life could arise.

NOTES

1. 1984 Directory of Lutheran Church of the Master, 6.

2. Most of the statistics are from the official yearbooks of the ALC from 1960 to 1987 and, after 1987, from the ELCA's yearbooks. (The number 359 is suspect because it is an increase of 93 over the previous year.)

3. Program/Facilities Task Force Report, 2.

4. Ibid., 4.

5. The gift to the ELCA established the "Lutheran Church of the Master Endowed Missionary Position." The gift to Luther Seminary proved doubly valuable, because it released $200,000 more in matching funds. And the gift to

Mount Carmel Ministries paid for the cost of a room in their new lodge that bears the congregation's name. It was satisfying to members to know that LCM's name would continue, even after the congregation dissolved.

6. Copies of the final services, final reports, and a longer history are available from: Region 3 Archives, Luther Seminary, 2481 Como Avenue, St. Paul, MN 55108.

PART 3

Resources for Leaders

12

The Value of Ritual:
Making Meaning, Forging Hope

Lucy Kolin

When the decision to close a congregation has been made, all sorts of primal but conflicting emotions and questions are set in motion. In this moment of chaos and distress, the use of ritual is essential and immediately available to help people of faith make meaning of a reality no one ever planned or imagined for their church. By "ritual," I mean commonly embraced symbols and regularly repeated patterns of words and actions. Ritual behavior is part of all human life and interaction; its daily uses often go unnoticed or are taken for granted. But when continuity is suddenly disrupted and the impossible is required of God's people, ritual becomes one of God's most precious gifts. And what does ritual do? Elaine Ramshaw writes in *Ritual and Pastoral Care* that ritual, in and beyond the church, offers individuals and communities a means to (1) establish order, (2) make or reaffirm meaning, (3) strengthen the bond of community, and (4) address and manage ambivalence.[1]

Perhaps a fifth function could be added, considering the particular focus of this book and chapter. When a congregation may feel like it is disappearing, when it appears its history of ministry is in danger of being erased from future memory, public ritual can provide the larger community— the larger church and the neighborhood, city, or town—an opportunity to acknowledge the contributions a particular congregation has made to the community, and to offer appreciation, thanks, and praise.

Using the Familiar to Heal the Unfamiliar

Until a community must face the question of whether and how to close, most congregations never consider that possibility. Certainly, it is not spoken of in the founding of a church, apart from the constitutional provisions required by the denomination and polity. So when the possibility and then the necessity arises, there is no sense of familiarity about it. And no one feels prepared to consider or to cope with the barrage of questions and emotions that assault individuals and the community as a whole.

When leaders consider what sort of worship befits a congregation's last days, therefore, it is tempting to think that something very different must be constructed to address and handle the newness and strangeness of the event. But the most effective and meaningful rituals are grounded in what is most familiar in a community's tradition—Word and Sacrament, familiar worship objects and appointments, hymns and prayers that have been taught to several generations, and the core theological tenets of providence, grace, forgiveness, and an eternally reliable God. Yes, new words and images and actions may indeed be called for, but to be most healing, they will need to be overlaid on the solid foundation of the familiar. Then they can open a way through the chaotic sea and reveal a path to the other side. And members will find courage to look forward and back and to believe in a new future as God's people in another expression or place.

Healing the Memories

The most obvious service associated with the dissolution of a congregation is the final, public closing service, which usually involves present members, former members, friends and neighbors from the community, area clergy and congregation members, and representatives of the local or next level judicatory. That service, for which many denominations offer a prototype, is more celebratory, even though grief is undoubtedly very present and active. Such a service might include a decommissioning of the congregation but end with a recommissioning of members for service in another congregation.

Many communities would also do well, however, to consider providing another sort of service or ritual prior to the public one, a service just for the "immediate family," the members of the congregation about to close.

In such a setting, feelings of sadness, anger, regret, and loss can be acknowledged and voiced more easily, and the release that follows words of forgiveness and healing can be appropriated more quickly.

In my first parish, Westlake Lutheran Church, Daly City, California, it was exactly this sort of ritual that freed the remaining members to release their bitterness, to hear each other say aloud that they were afraid they had not done all they could have to grow the church and its public ministry, and to voice anger at being abandoned by church officials, set adrift and declared as good as dead long before the decision to close was made.

The service we held was coupled with an evening meal and made full use of every part of the church property. We began in the kitchen area, where so many meals had been lovingly cooked and shared for 30 years. After a litany of thanksgiving (see the section on prayers), we ate a potluck meal of fellowship.

Then we moved to the social hall, where, under the compassionate leadership of a neighboring pastor, all—including me—engaged in a rite to "heal our memories." We said out loud in one another's presence what we thought we had done or left undone that may have contributed to the need to close. We acknowledged our anger and sadness at the ways others in our district and conference had refused or neglected us until it was too late. We asked for forgiveness for ourselves and for others, so that we might go forward free, forgiven, without bitterness or nagging resentments. We did so trusting that God would hear us and forgive and allow us to remember our dear church with gratitude, not regret, and to enter into the life of other congregations without the unhealthy "baggage" of unhealed anger and grief. What happened that evening was very healing. It also brought the blessed surprise of our neighboring pastor acknowledging that he and his congregation had been so fearful about what Westlake's possible dissolution might suggest about their own viability that they had stood back and watched instead of offering active support, including the broaching of a third way, the possibility of yoking or merger.

The healing of memories, simply a variation on a traditional rite of confession and absolution, culminated in the exchange of peace and was followed by our moving to the sanctuary to share the eucharist. As we walked back through the kitchen area and down the hallway into the church proper, we sang "Amazing Grace," for which no printed words were needed. Then we gathered around the altar, not in the pews, to celebrate what the program called the "meal of reconciliation and unity." The introduction and body of the communion prayer were both modified to fit the moment and the gathered body. So, for example, the introduction or preface began:

> In your great wisdom you called us together as Westlake Lutheran Church to proclaim your love and forgiveness to this community through Word and Sacrament and through the daily ministry of our lives. Now, as we complete this ministry, you promise to be with us still, calling us to new visions and new service.

And the prayer went on to speak of the local "mysterious fog" and to ask that "we who were once no people might ever remain your people."

The service concluded with a simple prayer and blessing. Former members still recall this service with gratitude and speak about the healing and release it provided. And the lives of energy, commitment, and cheerfulness they led in the congregations they joined following dissolution are eloquent testimony to the deep healing that those present experienced in this service.

Other Kinds of Rituals

There are special circumstances attached to every closing. These, too, are rightly addressed in ritual. For example, some congregations are able to designate the proceeds of the sale of their property, even when the real estate transaction will be handled by judicatory officials. Celebrating these last generous acts of stewardship and mission within the closing service can bring an almost palpable sense of power and hope, a little Easter out of the Good Friday of a congregation.

When Lutheran Church of the Master (ELCA), Bloomington, Minnesota, closed, a special service was held: "Service of Sowing Seeds for Mission." In the course of that service, representatives of various ministries and community agencies were present to receive the financial gifts the congregation voted to give them and to offer their public thanks and a brief statement about how those dollars would be translated into ministry and service. To do so meant that members of LCM and of their community could see and rejoice in the continuation of ministry and life their closing gifts would bring.

Highland Park Presbyterian Church, Minneapolis, celebrated "God doing a new thing" in a service that marked the end of one ministry and the establishment of a new ministry, Kwanzaa Fellowship. The service they wrote was divided into several "acts" that rehearsed with pride and thanksgiving the history of unfolding ministry and steadfast generosity, and celebrated the gifts of leadership Highland Park had offered to the greater church through missionaries and pastors sent into service by the congregation.

Denominations often provide rubrics and templates for services marking the disposition of church buildings, but the land itself is often neglected. Especially in rural communities, it may be particularly appropriate and consoling to create liturgies for acknowledging the blessing and cherishing of the land and then release it to other uses. A procession across the acreage, with various "stations" of remembrance and prayer along the way, could be a useful format. Prayers could be offered that acknowledge God as steward and sustainer of the land long after a worshiping community leaves. It would also be appropriate to pray for the next managers or occupants of the property, if they are known—and even to turn over the deed as part of the ritual. Where there is a gate or other clear entrance to the property, the final blessing and dismissal could take place there.

Suggested Scripture, Hymns, and Prayers

What has meaning for one congregation will be less meaningful for another. Choices for readings, hymns, and prayers are best made by a group of leaders from the congregation, including the pastoral staff. Suggestions, minimal or rich, for all of these appear in some of the worship resources of denominations, as in the ELCA's *Occasional Services: A Companion to Lutheran Book of Worship*. But contextualization is paramount. So leaders and planners might ask questions like these: What hymns have been most valued by the congregation? What scripture was read or preached at the founding or dedication? Did a particular hymn or scripture or prayer emerge as critical or helpful in the discernment process that led to a decision to close? Are there members gifted in poetry or song who, as part of their own healing process, might be invited to write hymns or prayers for the closing ritual? (Perhaps new words could be set to a treasured and familiar tune.) Might it help members and those who will gather to mark the closing to offer a litany or prayer based on the congregation's mission statement and so celebrate the ways that the Holy Spirit has worked fruitful ministry in and through the local church?

Still, it is good to know what scripture, hymns, and prayers have been meaningful to those who have experienced or created closing rituals. When feeling unsure how to begin or where to look for examples to stimulate one's own thinking about a ritual, it can be helpful to hear what has been meaningful to others who have had a similar experience. So, here are some suggestions gathered from people of several denominational and worship traditions who generously offer you their encouragement and prayers.

Scripture

Exodus 33:14, 15	God said, "My presence will go with you, and I will give you rest."
Deuteronomy 31:6	Be strong and bold; have no fear or dread, . . . because it is the Lord your God who goes with you, who will not fail you or forsake you.
1 Chronicles 17:16-22	[David said,] "Who am I, O Lord God, and what is my house, that you have brought me thus far?"
2 Samuel 7:18-29	[David said,] "Because of your promise, and according to your own heart, you have wrought all this greatness, so that your servant may know it. . . . Now therefore may it please you to bless the house of your servant, so that it may continue forever before you."
Psalm 13	How long, O Lord? Will you forget me forever? . . . But I trusted in your steadfast love.
Psalm 42	These things I remember, as I pour out my soul: how I went with the throng, and led them in procession to the house of God, with glad shouts and songs of thanksgiving.

Psalm 46:1-7	God is our refuge and strength, a very present help in trouble. Therefore, we will not fear, though the earth should change.
Psalm 74:2	Remember your congregation, which you acquired long ago.
Psalm 103	As for mortals, their days are like grass. . . . But the steadfast love of the Lord is from everlasting to everlasting on those who fear God.
Psalm 121	The Lord will keep your going out and your coming in from this time on and forevermore.
Ecclesiastes 3:1-8	For everything there is a season, and a time for every matter under heaven.
Isaiah 40:1-5	Comfort, O comfort my people, says your God.
Isaiah 43:1-4	But not thus says the Lord who created you, O Jacob, who formed you, O Israel. . . . I have called you by name, you are mine.
Matthew 16:24-28	Then Jesus told his disciples, "If any want to become my followers, let them deny themselves and take up their cross and follow me. For those who want to save their life will lose it, and those who lose their life for my sake will find it."
Mark 16:1-8	So they went out and fled from the tomb, for terror and amazement had seized them, and they said nothing to anyone for they were afraid.
John 14:1, 18-20, 27	[Jesus said,] "Do not let your hearts be troubled, . . . I will not leave you orphaned. . . . Peace I leave to you."

Romans 8:31-39	For I am convinced that neither death, nor life . . . will be able to separate us from the love of God in Christ Jesus our Lord.
Ephesians 4:4-6	There is one body and one Spirit, just as you were called to the one hope of your calling, one Lord, one faith, one baptism, one God and Father of all, who is above all and through all and in all.
Hebrews 1:10-12	But you are the same, and your years will never end.
Hebrews 13:8	Jesus Christ is the same yesterday and today and forever.
1 Peter 2:4-10	Come to Christ, a living stone . . . and like living stones let yourselves be built into a spiritual house. . . . Once you were not a people, but now you are God's people.
Revelation 21:1-4, 22-27	And I heard a loud voice from the throne saying, "See, the home of God is among mortals. . . . God will wipe every tear from their eyes. . . . mourning and crying and pain will be no more. . . ." Its [the city's] gates will never be shut by day—and there will be no night there.

Other scripture might be selected from the lessons read on the day the church was founded or dedicated. One might also consider the scripture featured in the congregation's mission statement or inscribed on its cornerstone, on its walls, or over its doors. A new layer of consoling meaning can be uncovered when familiar scripture is read in a time such as this.

The liturgical churches follow a three-year lectionary cycle, while other churches expect that preachers will be led to texts and messages that reflect the immediate life and struggles of the congregation. However texts are chosen for the Lord's Day, for every worship service that precedes the final service, the preacher needs to preach in a way that encourages honesty, repentance, mutual consolation, and faith in God's providence and Easter.

In some ways, this is no different from the usual preaching task. In the time between the decision to close and the formal dissolution of a congregation, however, there is a great vulnerability afoot in the church. The proclamation of the word, then, must take care not to "break the bruised reed" or "quench the dimly burning wick." Frequent conversation with members can open a preacher's eyes to the ways of speaking that can console and also reinvigorate faith and hope.

Hymns

[*Authors of texts are indicated.*]
"Now Thank We All Our God" (*Martin Rinckhart*)
"Praise to the Lord, the Almighty, the King of Creation" (*Joachim Neander*)
"Amazing Grace" (*John Newton*)
"A Mighty Fortress Is Our God" (*Martin Luther*)
"My Hope Is Built on Nothing Less" (*Edward Mote*)
"Blest Be the Tie That Binds" (*John Fawcett*)
"The Church's One Foundation" (*Samuel Wesley*)
"Blessed Assurance" (*Fanny Crosby*)
"God of Grace and God of Glory" (*Harry Fosdick*)
"O God, Our Help in Ages Past" (*Isaac Watts*)
"The Church of Christ in Every Age" (*F. Pratt Green*)
"For All the Saints" (*William How*)
"Lift High the Cross" (*George Kitchin; Michael Newbolt*)
"Praise God from Whom All Blessings Flow" (*Thomas Ken*)[2]
"For Many Years, O God of Grace" (*William Czamanske*)
"Blest Be the Dear Uniting Love" (*Charles Wesley*)
"We Know That Christ Is Raised" (*John Geyer*)
"In the Bulb There Is a Flower" (*Natalie Sleeth*)
"If You But Trust in God to Guide You" (*Georg Neumark*)
"We Love Your Realm, O God" (*Timothy Dwight; adapted by Lavon Bayler*)
"Go, My Children, with My Blessing" (*Jaroslav Vajda*)
"Healer of Our Every Ill" (*Marty Haugen*)
"Stay with Us" (*Herbert Brokering*)
"Bind Us Together" (*Bob Gillman*)
"Great Is Thy Faithfulness" (*Thomas Chisholm*)
"On Our Way Rejoicing" (*John Monsell*)
"God Be with You till We Meet Again" (*Jeremiah Rankin*)

Worship planners might also want to consider using hymns and anthems written especially for the congregation, perhaps for its founding or for an anniversary. Former choir members might be invited to come together and sing a simple, favorite anthem. It is also possible to adapt classic hymns written for church anniversaries, changing present tenses to past where needed.

Such hymns can help us remember the all-encompassing and multigenerational ministry of our congregations; they can translate into another sort of praise psalm for God's deeds of love and blessing carried out through the church.

Perhaps as another means of encouragement, someone might be invited to write a hymn or anthem for the closing service. No one expects to receive gifts at the death of a congregation, but, given our theology, perhaps we should. Such a specially composed hymn would testify to the grace of a God who always gives good gifts, especially to those who are languishing and empty.

Prayers

There is beauty in prayers that are formal and ancient, a sturdiness and security that gives us courage to pray about hard times and difficult matters. In some denominations that provide explicit rites and liturgies for the closing of congregations, there will be appointed prayers. Some are provided below.

But there is also beauty and meaning in prayers composed by the people of the congregation and their worship leaders. Such prayers will be highly contextual; they will speak the language of today's community. Their language can make possible the naming of particular feelings present in the hearts of the worshipers. They can be specifically about the history and fruits of ministry in that place. A few such prayers are referenced or included here to inspire your own.

Where networks of prayer already are established in a congregation, leaders may want to call for the praying of a common prayer daily, leading up to a vote for dissolution or the final service. This solidarity of conversation with God and intercession for one another may provide a special comfort and strength.

One excellent idea that comes from Pastor Lindsay Biddle, another contributor to this book, involves creating a litany that incorporates themes or direct statements from the mission statement of the congregation. For example, "We will worship, study, engage in fellowship and mission together" from the mission statement became "We give thanks to God for the worship, study, fellowship and mission we have engaged in together." Pastor Biddle remembers that the litany was received well because "the members were familiar with the statement and recognized the words and phrases." It enabled them to lift up to God with glad remembrance and thanksgiving all the work and energy they had experienced and expressed over the years.

Of course, as befits a congregation's worship practices and traditions, time can be left for the particular voiced and silent prayers of those gathered, so that all that calls out to be prayed for may find a place.

Many Protestant traditions give great weight to the spoken word and thus, to spoken prayer, spontaneous or composed. Perhaps at a time when so much ambivalence, so many conflicting emotions and thoughts are present in the body of Christ, it would be good—if it is not too unfamiliar—to include other modes of prayer, whether danced prayer, chants, visualizations, or simply silence into which the Spirit can speak.

Prayer for the Fifth Sunday of Easter
(Lutheran and Episcopal Communions)

O God, form the minds of your faithful people into a single will . . . .

A Prayer after Communion
(Adapted from Martin Luther's Post-Communion Prayer)

We give you thanks, Almighty God, that you have refreshed us through the healing power of this gift of life, as you have refreshed those before us who have received your Word and Holy Sacraments in this place. Turn our sorrow over the closing of this congregation into joy over new opportunities for life and ministry in other congregations. In your mercy, strengthen us and your whole church in faith toward you and in fervent love toward one another; for the sake of Jesus Christ our Lord. Amen

A Prayer after Communion
(For the Closing Service of Westlake Lutheran Church)

We thank you, dear God, for this meal that we have shared, this meal that brings peace and the promise of new and lasting life to your people. Deepen in us the vision of hope in what is yet to come, that we may find in every change and happening not an ending but a promise, the sign of your new creation in ourselves and in our world. We pray in Jesus' name. Amen

A Litany of Thanksgiving
(Based on a Traditional Passover Seder song)

L: Great and numerous are the kindnesses that the Lord has extended to us; for each of them we offer thanks and humble gratitude.

C: Any one of these would have been sufficient to show God's love for us, God's pity and compassion.

L: Had God done nothing more than call us by name and make of us the people of God,

C: For that alone we should be grateful!

L: Had God done nothing more than build this congregation and empower it for __ years of ministry,

C: For that alone we should be grateful!

L: Had God done nothing more than give us pastors and teachers, parents and leaders who spoke God's word with spirit and compassion,

C: For that alone we should be grateful!

L: Had God done nothing more than give to us the very gifts we needed— gifts to care for the house of God, gifts to care for the people of God—

C: For that alone we should be grateful!

L: Had God done nothing more than give us each other to love, to serve, to comfort and sustain in the spirit of Christ,

C: For that alone we should be grateful!

L: How great and numerous are the kindnesses that the Lord has shown us! For all these gifts, we gladly say:

C: Thanks be to God! Amen!

Final Thoughts

Different churches have different sacramental understandings and practices, but in any of them the continued offering of the sacraments can bring hope and blessing. Communion offers forgiveness and healing, strengthens faith, and builds us up as the body of Christ. Bread and wine shared also reminds us that we are connected without interruption to God and through God with one another. Congregations are organized and close, and church members nowadays may move into and out of several congregations in a lifetime, but all who confess Jesus as Lord are united through baptism in a life that has no geographic or temporal limits.

Through the traditional and familiar, as well as through the "something new" in a congregation's life, God promises to be at work . . . always. In many and various ways the one who is our Emmanuel is indeed with us, leading us through the waters of chaos to a new and promised land. Thanks be to God!

NOTES

1. Elaine Ramshaw, *Ritual and Pastoral Care* (Philadelphia: Fortress Press, 1987).

2. To the traditional doxology might be added verses written by Lavon Baylor and included in *Refreshing Rains of the Living Word* (New York: The Pilgrim Press, 1988).

13

Congregational Records and Artifacts

Paul Daniels

People who have shared a place of worship have stories to tell about their life together. In one way or another the members of these communities entrust their story to physical records, such as paper, film, and magnetic tape. Congregations also show the observer what is important in their worship, education, and fellowship through media other than the expected forms of paper and microfilm. Altar paraments, vestments, stained-glass windows, two- and three-dimensional art objects, and sanctuary furniture are examples of what scholars call "material culture." These conveyors of story are more difficult to quantify and evaluate than the paper records that deliver data in more or less straightforward ways. Both physical documents and church artifacts, however, play a critical role in the act of remembering congregational life.

This act of recalling the life and mission of our churches is an important and enriching activity of a congregation. When a congregation closes, in effect ending that community's mission in the world, the role of records and artifacts (the objects around us in our churches) takes on even greater significance. This is why nearly all services for the closing of a congregation include an actual passing on of the record books to the next congregation where the majority of members will attend or to the next judicatory level charged with this responsibility by the denomination. While on one level this act simply represents good record-keeping practices, on a deeper level, obvious to those people whose church is closing, such ritual action is the very real passing on of the vehicles of memory to safekeeping in the new setting.

Preparing Congregational Records

Most congregations facing closure have many more pressing issues facing them than determining final placement of their records and artifacts. It is ironic, then, that these materials will prove of such value later, when the closure is complete and members of that congregation as well as the wider church begin to take the time to remember the full range of life in that congregation. In fact, some of the church's most important records will be produced in the waning days of the congregation's life, including property disposition papers and correspondence with denominational officials about the closure.

Some churches are already prepared for this day by maintaining an active archives or heritage committee. Some even have a congregational historian whose responsibilities include the collection and care of the congregation's historical records. Generally, if a congregation has maintained this level of attention to its records, the decisions around final disposition of materials will be more easily made. Ideally, of course, disposition decisions have been anticipated in this way, but what is the congregation to do if this has not been the case?

The good news is that even as the formal closure date approaches, it is still not too late to do the right thing with the congregation's documented memory. The tasks of inventorying existing records, locating misplaced items of permanent value, and determining an overall retention plan are all activities supported by experts within our major denominations. In short, the closing congregation does not need to go through this process alone. Whether decisions about documents and artifacts are handled by church staff persons such as the minister or the church secretary, or volunteer lay people serving on a closure committee, denominational services are generally available at little or no cost. In fact, the advice about records retention and artifact care found on the Web sites of seven major denominations is open for use by anyone. In addition, a number of these church bodies provide services to congregations on a simple cost-recovery basis. Several of the denominational Web sites surveyed indicated services such as microfilming church records and storing records from closed churches are available to the denomination's congregations at minimal cost.

Part of the preparation for the care of records when a congregation is preparing to close involves creating an inventory of the existing records, whether they are in an archival collection or simply part of the church office filing system. Preferably, the work group includes the church secretary or someone else who is well acquainted with the filing system of the church office. If this is not possible, the committee should include people with good organizational skills and the patience and the persistence to complete the task.

A priority for this group will be locating the records themselves. When this has been done, they will need to find a secure place in the church building where the ongoing work of sorting records can be done. Sorting does not need to be a particularly complex or involved process. The first task is to form groups of "like" material; for example, vestry records belong with other vestry records. Within this record group, the papers should be organized chronologically. It is best to maintain the original order of records when possible.

During the sorting process, gaps in the records will become obvious. It is critical that valuable materials like the parish register or pastor's book, including records of baptisms, marriages, funerals, and other such official acts, are complete. This is a good time to solicit missing materials from likely sources in the congregation. In general, it is best to ask for specific items or types of items rather than to simply ask the congregation for old records. Not only is the committee more likely to receive the needed material, but congregation members will begin to see that care and concern are being given to the task of story preservation.

Appraisal of Records

Even while the sorting process is underway, whether they are conscious of it or not, the committee members will be making decisions about the relative value of materials. In fact, they will be performing the appraisal task necessary in all archives work. In formal archival practice standards are applied to materials to guide decisions on retention or destruction of records. These same criteria can be applied to church records. The Web site of the Presbyterian Historical Society (www.history.pcusa.org) presents four appraisal measures particularly well. It suggests determining value of records by asking what fiscal, legal, administrative, and historical significance they have.

Records that possess fiscal importance will be needed by the closing church, both in the short term and in the long term. These would include annual audits, property papers and contracts, and papers filed with the government for tax purposes. Records having to do with the closing itself, for example, the sale of property or fulfillment of certain contracts, should be kept permanently.

Closely related are materials of legal importance. These would include constitution and bylaws, articles of incorporation, and other documents needed to establish, or to prove after the fact, the existence of a congregation. Because there is sometimes significant variation among states regarding record-keeping requirements for nonprofit organizations such as churches, it is wise to check with local authorities or an attorney before destroying legal papers.

The next appraisal value, administrative, will cover the largest number of church records. In essence, these records show how the church organization functioned and changed over time. They will include agenda, minutes, and related material of the representative body governing the church (the council, board, vestry, or session). Arguably, this material could also have legal and financial value. Additionally, all congregations produce records on their individual members. These membership records are usually in a bound book or notebook—variously called the membership book, the pastor's book, or book of ministerial acts. Containing baptism, marriage, confirmation, funeral, transfer, and installation information, these records are among the most precious any church possesses. They need to be kept permanently.

Finally, there is the category of historical significance. Of the four, this is the most subjective measurement and in many ways the most important, because this is where the stories of people in mission and ministry are lodged. When judging the permanent historical content of records, it is important to be open to the stories they contain, sometimes found just below the surface. Accordingly, even materials as seemingly straightforward, if not downright dull, as committee minutes and reports can contain the narrative elements of the congregation's story. With careful reading and a sense of their storytelling potential, congregation members can lay claim to their shared faith stories through their own records. Good examples of such records are older reports and minutes of the women's auxiliary organization or similar material for the Christian education program. These activities tend to be particularly well documented.

Visual materials, such as photographs, videotapes, and films, also possess significant historical value. Most churches have wonderful examples of these in the form of confirmation, baptism, and wedding photographs.

Other images depict women at work in various church tasks or large, informal group gatherings. Both provide valuable social and cultural information as well as information about the congregational history. The committee working with archival records will need to consider how to handle undated and unidentified images, for while the picture may still tell us something, its value is decreased by the lack of verifiable information. This factor needs to be considered when determining permanent retention.

Considering Options

What is the closing congregation to do, then, with what could be a large inventory of paper, films, tape, and disks? The ideal solution would be simply to transfer the lot to either the next congregation where most members are joining or to the synod, district, diocese, or circuit office. Neither is a viable option. It is hard to imagine any church, and certainly any denominational office, having enough space for long-term storage. The closing congregation will simply have to reduce the volume of materials planned for permanent retention.

Using the four appraisal criteria as general guidelines and the resources available through denominational archivists, it is possible to develop a manageable and useful list of needed records. Among helpful Web sites are those of the Presbyterian Historical Society (www.history.pcusa.org), the Southern Baptist Historical Library and Archives (www.sbhla.org), the Archives of the Episcopal Church (www.episcopalarchives.org), the General Commission on Archives and History of the United Methodist Church (www.gcah.org), and the Office of the Secretary of the Evangelical Lutheran Church in America (www.elca.org). The Roman Catholic Church and its dioceses also have helpful Web sites. Presumably, the process of closure and the disposition of records is handled by provisions of canon law and with considerable involvement of the bishop and his staff.

Developing a List of Records

Archivists often recommend various retention periods (often one year, five years, 10 years, and then transfer or destruction are proposed), but for closing congregations, the assumption must be that permanent retention of a reasonable amount of material is the goal. There will not be another time like the period leading up to the closing to work as knowledgeably with the records, so care needs to be taken to consider the records as a whole.

The following checklist of materials to be retained, compiled from materials from various denominations, is a guide for congregations facing closure.

1. Articles of incorporation, constitution, and bylaws
2. Membership records of baptism, marriage, confirmation, funerals, and other official acts
3. Minutes of governing board meetings
4. Minutes of full congregational meetings, regular and special
5. Minutes of other committees and auxiliary groups. (Retain as much as storage space permits. Consider sampling collections if space is limited.)
6. Congregational newsletters
7. Worship service bulletins
8. Property papers, titles, and deeds
9. All insurance policies (including expired policies)
10. Annual audit reports
11. Statistics as reported to judicatory offices
12. Printed histories for anniversaries and other significant events
13. Congregational directories
14. Visual and audio records: photographs and negatives, films and tape
15. Church cemetery records

Sampling to Reduce Record Collections' Size

Once materials have been inventoried and their approximate value determined, as number 5 above suggests, decisions must be made about what specific items to keep. The size of items and the availability of storage space must be taken into consideration. If it is clear that certain groups of records meet a number of the appraisal criteria for retention but storage space is limited, sampling is a good option. To do this, one simply selects every third or every fifth item (or whatever number seems to provide the representative sample from the whole) for retention. The remaining files are destroyed. The main benefit of sampling is that it reduces the total number of records while maintaining the records' presence in the overall collection. This process works best with large amounts of material of considerable, but perhaps not ultimate, value. Sampling is also a good way of dealing with large collections that contain unneeded duplicate material. Examples include the minutes of auxiliary groups, such as the church choir, altar guild, or women's organization. It is not necessary to save everything, because not every item is of equal value.

Microfilming for Preservation

Microfilming is another way to reduce the size of archival collections. Ideally, microfilming records supplements the original set of records by providing a back-up copy for preservation purposes while the paper set is retained. It may be necessary, however, to reduce a large collection to microfilm when storage space is inadequate. Examples of materials to be microfilmed would be records, the congregational newsletter, and service bulletins. While these tend to take up considerable storage space and might be considered disposable when a congregation is closing, they are also the two most valuable sets of records for documenting day-to-day congregational life. Microfilming these records would be time and money well spent, because microfilming remains one of the most affordable, reliable, and durable of preservation processes.

Moving information to microfilm eliminates the need to convert data as computer software changes. When a congregation closes, it is doubtful that anyone will step forward to oversee continual conversion of electronically stored records, making a stable format like microfilm even more attractive. In addition, even if information has been scanned or stored in other electronic forms, the technology exists to move this information to a microfilm format.

Artifacts and Their Care

Even more than record material, church artifacts present unique storage problems. All churches have objects of varying kinds that convey aspects of the congregation's story, though perhaps somewhat less directly than the archival records discussed above. These items can range from wooden pews and other sanctuary furniture to stained glass windows and altar vessels. These pieces are not like objects we use in daily life. We have given them sacred significance, making decisions about their further care particularly important. One helpful way to begin the decision process is offered by the Presbyterian Historical Society Web site. The site suggests determining which items had sacred importance; that is, which were used in worship settings. Items that were not used in worship can be given away to members or donated to a local historical society. They could also be sold, with the proceeds becoming part of a legacy gift for the sacred items' care in a denominational collection (an idea suggested by the Disciples of Christ history site).

Artifacts such as vestments, paraments, baptismal fonts, and communion ware are of real concern for closing congregations. In many cases denominational judicatories are able to suggest mission churches or camping ministries that need these kinds of artifacts. Several denominations are willing to advertise the availability of sacred objects in their newsletters or general mailings. This can be an effective way of connecting closing congregations and their objects with other congregations or church organizations in need of these sacred pieces. Ideally, churches would have access to an integrated national database listing sacred objects available. At this writing, such an ecumenical list does not exist, so it is still best for the closing congregation to work with its denominational judicatory body on both archives and artifacts questions.

The Closing Congregation and Its Church Body

Finally, a few words need to be said about the congregation and its relationship to its denomination at the time of closure. The closing congregation will be well served by the information available from its denomination's office of records management and archives. In general, the denominations known for congregational autonomy, such as the United Church of Christ, the Disciples of Christ, and certain of the Baptist groups, grant a higher level of congregational choice in disposition of records. While some of these congregations may choose to deposit their records with the nearest UCC or Disciples church, or with the congregation where most members are transferring, it often makes practical sense to have the records remain near the people who created them. Other congregations may deposit their records with the judicatory's archive or with a state historical society.

In general, it is best for closing congregations to remain in close contact with the church body office and to seek the advice of its archivists and records managers.

On the other end of the polity spectrum are church bodies such as the Roman Catholic Church that exercise considerable influence on closure decisions. Churches of these traditions will find that determining what needs to be saved and where materials are to be deposited are fairly straightforward tasks. In most cases, the records are automatically transferred to the diocesan archives at the time of closure.

Somewhere between these poles are denominations such as Lutherans (ELCA, Lutheran Church—Missouri Synod, and other Lutheran groups), the United Methodist Church, and the Presbyterian Church (U.S.A.). These groups work with the understanding that closing congregations will use the appropriate denominational archives for final disposition of their records, assuming that the records have not been transferred to the nearest custodial church of the same denomination. If records are not turned over to another congregation, then the closing congregation should notify the church archives of the records' location. In no case should the records stay in an individual's home. Denominational archives maintain files on congregations and need information such as closure date, location of records, and disposition of artifacts. This information can be invaluable to future researchers and will ensure that the closed congregation's story lives on.

Congregations anticipating closure have a rich resource in their denominational office and archives staff. There is no need to go it alone with decisions about records retention, care of artifacts, and final storage locations. The denominational Web sites are a wonderful place to begin, but a letter or telephone call will also connect the closing church to professional staff people eager to help pass the congregation's story along to the next generation.

14

Deciding What to Do with the Building

Jennifer Lynn Baskerville

Closing a congregation is arguably one of the most difficult decisions a worshiping congregation will ever face. As a community of faith wrestles with an often uncertain though possibly transformational future, it can be very easy to leave out the biggest asset: the building. Although there will be much grieving to be done over the loss of a congregational family, it is wise to anticipate and make room for the grief that accompanies the loss of the building. When a congregation closes and leaves a building behind, the concept of being spiritually homeless takes on literal meaning.

In the following pages we will explore the issues related to grieving and leaving the congregational home. In many cases, a congregation can avoid additional grief by decreasing the likelihood that their worship space will be demolished or reused in a disrespectful way. But first, let us take a look at why one should consider the building in this leave-taking process at all.

Building Theology

One of the hallmarks of Christianity is the notion that the "church" is not a place but a people. The church is to be found wherever God's people are, and the presence of God is not dictated or limited by a physical location. In his book on Christian sacred spaces, *The House of God*, Edward Norman writes:

The Church is a condition of things, not a building. To examine a church structure, therefore . . . is to contemplate the material evidence of a reality which is invisibly present. It is to see the imperfect description of faith, not its substance. But it is, nevertheless, to sense something of the spiritual splendor which the world anticipates and which, Christians believe, eternity delivers.[1]

One of the realities of faith communities, however, is that the worship, fellowship, education, and community outreach of a congregation takes place in buildings—usually grand, artful, and emotionally and architecturally significant buildings. While these buildings do not capture the presence of God, they do serve as the place where a community can locate its encounters with the divine. Therefore, a house of worship is not just a building, but is indeed sacred space. Churches are the places new members are initiated, couples are wed, and loved ones are memorialized. Religious buildings are the silent guests at these events and many other sacred life events. By playing this role over the course of generations, religious buildings become part of the sacred history of a community. So although a church, synagogue, or temple can never be described as just "the building," it is never "just another building" for those who worship there.

The Church Building as a Member of the Community

Likewise, because religious properties are often among the most striking and notable buildings in any community, they are rarely "just another building" for those in the larger community—even those who have no claim on it. Religious buildings are often among the most prominent landmarks in any community. The visual images of many cities and towns are given definition by the steeples and domes punctuating their landscape. Houses of worship are often appreciated by the greater community as places that offer symbolic stability, aesthetic nourishment, and a sense of historic and architectural legacy. Cities such as Buffalo or Brooklyn, New York, and the rural town greens of Vermont have similar stories to tell about how church steeples and temple domes not only tell a story about the community, but help give the landscape its identity.

On a more practical level, it has been well documented that religious properties contribute significantly to community life through the space they offer for childcare programs, arts programs, and meeting spaces for various recovery and self-help groups. Most communities would be at a loss to house such programs were religious properties to cease providing space for them.

Many congregations underestimate the full impact their building may have on the community at large. When the First Baptist Church in Morristown, New Jersey, suffered extensive damage from a fire in May 2000, the small congregation was amazed by the outpouring of community support from both the religious and nonreligious communities. Some of that support may have been offered because the community feared losing the oldest church building in Morristown. But it is more likely that the community recognized the contributions First Baptist made by housing several critical and significant programs for the homeless and hungry in the Morristown area. Now, First Baptist is doing what would not have been possible on its own: with the help of the community it is nearing the completion of a rebuilding campaign.

Grieving the Loss of the Building

Other chapters in this volume that speak to the loss a congregation will experience in its dissolution and the rituals that may help the grieving process. As a congregation grieves for what it is no longer, members may find it helpful and appropriate to remember to grieve for the building as well. When a congregation leaves a building behind, members do not leave God behind, but do leave behind identity-shaping history and memory. Religious buildings are usually packed with reminders of and memorials to those who have gone before. Some of these artifacts can be removed from the building for safekeeping. Many other treasures, however, such as altars, stained-glass windows, and other sacred furniture may need to be left behind or in some way sensitively dealt with.

The congregation or judicatory entrusted with the closing of a church should anticipate well in advance how these sacred objects are to be handled. Sometimes, features such as windows are left behind in the building because their ongoing care and a lack of proper storage dictate that course of action. Several options are available for other items, such as memorial books and plaques, silver, and other appointments, however. They can be given to historical societies or local history museums. Sometimes, many such artifacts are returned to the families that donated or commissioned them. Very often, objects such as altars, vestments, and candelabra are sold or given away to other congregations that might be able to use them so that they retain their purpose. In all cases, records should be kept of the deaccessioning of these objects, noting what went where in case the items should ever need to be recollected. This dispersal process should be part of the early leave-taking work, so that it is not done with last-minute haste.

Because worship spaces are usually set apart or consecrated for their special use, it may be appropriate in some traditions to arrange for a ceremony of deconsecration. Deconsecration ceremonies are usually conducted by religious leaders to free up a sacred space for nonreligious use. These rituals do not, of course, remove the sacred history and memory from a place, but they help the community understand that it is no longer set apart for the sacred.

Selling the Building

When a congregation or judicatory reaches the point when it is necessary to sell its building, it will find that selling a religious property will present unique circumstances and more difficult challenges than most other building types. The primary challenge for those faced with the task of selling a church, synagogue, temple, or mosque is to find a buyer who will, at the very least, use the building in a manner that respects the building's integrity and history, and retains its presence in the community landscape.

By far, the most sensitive (and often more comforting) option is to sell the building to another religious group. Most often, worship places that are sold are purchased by other congregations, denominations, or faiths. Because religious practice in any community is so greatly determined by demographic shifts, many towns and cities can tell at least one story about a religious building that is owned and used by a denomination or faith other than the one that constructed it. It is not uncommon to find Baptist congregations worshiping in former Lutheran churches or to find Presbyterian churches transformed into Greek or Serbian Orthodox houses of worship.

These sales can be negotiated between congregations or between judicatories in arrangements that are most often pleasing to all parties. Often, such sales occur long after the congregation has left, leaving it to luck that another religious body will buy the property and use it respectfully.

Whether the sacred space is sold to another religious group or to a secular entity, there are options for protecting the future of the building.

Adaptive Reuse Options

Although the majority of religious properties are sold to other religious groups, for reasons related to demographics, zoning laws, and the vagaries of real estate, many are not. In these cases, houses of worship are often sold for an adaptive reuse. "Adaptive reuse" describes a building project in which a structure originally constructed for one use is made usable for a different purpose or program.

The options for reusing houses of worship are plentiful. Not all of the options available, however, are necessarily the most sensitive or respectful of the building. Cases involving the conversion of churches in New York City and Miami into dance clubs are well known. Most constituencies concerned about religious properties—congregations, judicatories, and in the case of older and historic buildings, preservation organizations—will have an interest in the continued use and maintenance of these buildings. Some new uses, however, will be harmful to the architectural integrity of the structure and will do more harm than good to an important building.

When a congregation or judicatory sells a house of worship, normally the new owner has the ability to do whatever it pleases with the structure. A new owner could subdivide the sanctuary space and replace priceless windows. With foresight, however, the owners of a church or synagogue may have great influence over what happens to the property once it is sold. Of course, a congregation may decide to entertain only those bids that are in agreement with its desires for the building. But this is no long-term guarantee of appropriate use. The only way to ensure respectful use of the building is to establish covenants with the new owners placing restrictions on what changes can be made to the structure.

In many instances, the intentions or hopes of those looking to buy and reuse a religious property will be limited by the structure itself. A developer might want to use the building for a theater or music hall, for example, but the existing configuration of spaces may not be conducive to a conversion of that type. The type and amount of ornamentation, stained glass, and woodwork may present special challenges, and the layout of rooms and circulation spaces may not permit some uses. In some churches, those with a complex configuration of bearing walls, for instance, the redesign of spaces, may become difficult and expensive. These same issues will be of concern to potential buyers, who may be interested in the location and design of the structure but find the conversion too expensive even if they can afford to pay the purchase price.

For the most part, every type of new use presents its own unique set of challenges. In the remaining pages, a variety of uses will be considered. They represent the most frequently used conversion types and reflect the broad range of possibilities available. Congregations and judicatories looking to sell their building will want to consider these possibilities within the context of their geographic and cultural location.

Cultural and Arts Facilities

Next to conversions for use by other denominations or faiths, the adaptation of a house of worship for cultural and arts facilities represents the most natural and common option for worship spaces. Because they were built to serve as a place for public assembly, relatively little work may be required for them to accommodate performance art programs such as music, drama, and dance. Houses of worship also typically contain the variety of spaces needed for visual arts facilities such as galleries and exhibit spaces.

Adaptation for cultural arts facilities also provide a link to the building's original use. Many thriving congregations already use their worship spaces as forums for plays, readings, and musical performances. In some theological traditions, worship is understood as a sacred dance. In others, known for their emphasis on preaching, worship places were designed to be oratories, so that all could see the worship leader; every seat was a good seat. The transition from sacred to secular space in these instances is thus an easy one, both physically and philosophically.

Physically, these facilities usually have certain requirements not normally met in standard houses of worship. Performance facilities will generally need to be equipped with more rest rooms than would exist in a typical church, synagogue, or mosque. Lobby space and a ticket window are also crucial elements. In addition, these spaces are required by law to be handicapped accessible (depending on the capacity of the building). Usually, the worship space, basement, and other ancillary rooms will be sufficient for meeting the most basic needs of a performance facility.

Gallery/Exhibition Space

Houses of worship have traditionally been places where art—paintings, murals, tapestries, and sculpture—has been displayed and enjoyed. Adapting a worship space for use as a visual arts facility is in many ways much simpler than developing a performance facility. Whether it is adapted for use as a gallery, museum, or community art center, this type of conversion is amenable to almost any size worship space without requiring elaborate or specialized spaces. The tall ceilings and unobstructed seating areas of most houses of worship are ideal for exhibition spaces. Depending on the art media intended for display, the conversion will usually only entail removal of seating and the installation of appropriate heating, ventilating, air conditioning, and security systems.

The size of the building will often dictate the size of the arts program that may be possible. Multigalleried museums will be more appropriate in larger structures, while smaller houses of worship may be just right for a gallery space with changing exhibits. Community arts centers will work in almost any size structure.

Another option in this category is the house of worship as museum, in which case very few changes are made and the building itself is the exhibit, telling the history of a particular congregation or community. The Museum of Afro American History in Boston, Massachusetts, in one example. The cost of this adaptive use was mostly for the renovation and restoration of the structure itself. The interior of the church was restored to a particular point in time, and exhibit cases illustrate the history of the church and congregation using period photographs and artifacts. Because it is a part of the Afro American History Trail, the structure is tied into the history of the larger community as well.

Libraries

Houses of worship can make fine accommodations for a library. The large open space of the worship area is often perfect for use as a reading room and stack placement. This use can work in a variety of geographic locations. The small town of Carver, Minnesota, converted an Episcopal church into the town's public library. The location of houses of worship may make them ideal for this kind of use, as they are, with the exception of very rural congregations, usually located in town centers, residential areas, or other accessible areas.

Schools and Academies

Houses of worship located in downtown areas, in small towns, or cities may also be ideal for reuse by schools and academies. For churches and synagogues located near colleges, universities, and preparatory schools, academic use can be a viable option. Academic institutions are often drawn to houses of worship as potential reuse projects because of the architectural design of the structure, often adding interest to the institution's own collection of buildings. More importantly, converting a worship space for academic use may entail few, but critical, modifications. Usually, the worship area makes for an excellent lecture hall, and any ancillary spaces such as fellowship halls, classrooms, and offices can be used for seminar rooms. The classrooms and offices can retain their original purpose.

There are many other viable options for adaptively reusing sacred spaces, including dance facilities, community activity centers, and even recreational facilities. One of the best ways a congregation can preserve the legacy its building leaves behind is to carefully consider the possible uses for the property.

Key Questions to Ask When Undertaking This Process

The painful process of closing a congregation and selling its buildings can present a dizzying array of options and challenges. This final section presents some questions a congregation or judicatory might find helpful when deciding what will best serve the interests of the congregation and the building it leaves behind. This list of questions is by no means exhaustive but is meant to be a launching pad for other considerations that will be particular to each context and situation.

* Make sure everyone is clear on who owns the property. Is it the congregation or the judicatory? Who makes the final decisions about what happens to the building?

- Does the congregation or judicatory have a full understanding of the physical condition of the building? Is a property or conditions assessment planned?
- Though limited financial resources may make it difficult, is there a plan for maintaining or making improvements on the building before the congregation vacates it?
- If the judicatory retains ownership of the building after the congregation has left, is there a plan for continued maintenance and care?
- Are there any local or national landmark designations on the building, or is the building located in a landmark district?
- Has the congregation or judicatory been given the opportunity to think about and discuss what the building means to them?
- Have the pastoral care issues related to the building departure been anticipated and addressed?
- Are sacred places included in the conversations about stewardship? If not, how might the care and disposition of religious properties be understood as a stewardship issue?
- Has the congregation or judicatory learned about and discussed the philosophy or theology of sacred places? Is there agreement? What are the points of disagreement or tension?
- Has an inventory of memorial gifts, historical artifacts, and priceless treasures been conducted?
- What is the plan for disbursal of these objects?
- Does the congregation or judicatory have an indication of the building's value to the community? Organizations such as Partners for Sacred Places can help with such an assessment.
- Are there plans for conversations with community residents and community leaders, such as those involved in human services, culture and the arts, neighborhood development, and historic preservation? These conversations, especially when conducted early in the process, may be valuable to preserving the house of worship should it ever become endangered.
- Does your tradition have rituals for saying good-bye to the building, such as deconsecration ceremonies?

The closing of a congregation and the sale of its sacred buildings can be just as painful as any other grief process. Indeed, losing a faith community and its worship space can be akin to losing a loved one and having to sell the family home. In both cases, those who mourn should be aware of the many sources of support available to them. Chapter 15 in this volume will provide some of the many resources available to congregations and judicatories as they plan for and go about the difficult work of moving their buildings into what we hope will be a new phase of life.

NOTES
Portions of this chapter were adapted from an unpublished text by the author that was written under the auspices of Partners for Sacred Places.

1. Edward Norman, *The House of God: Church Architecture, Style and History* (London: Thames and Hudson Ltd., 1990), 7.

15

Guidance for Decision Makers

Partners for Sacred Places

PARTNERS FOR SACRED PLACES
1700 Sansom Street, 10th Floor
Philadelphia, PA 19103-5215
(215) 567-3234
fax: (215) 567-3235
partners@sacredplaces.org
www.sacredplaces.org

Partners for Sacred Places is the national center for the preservation and stewardship of older and historic religious properties. Since its founding in 1989, Partners has assisted thousands of community leaders and congregations in their efforts to keep their sacred places active in service to the community.

Partners' resources, which include *The Complete Guide to Capital Campaigns for Historic Churches and Synagogues* and its Information Clearinghouse, can help a congregation plan a simple restoration project, undertake a complex fund-raising campaign, or find new ways to use its assets to fulfill its mission and serve the community. Partners also has resources for congregations looking for creative ideas for their old buildings, including adaptive reuse and shared use with other organizations.

Partners advocates for sacred places on a national level by promoting a new understanding of how churches, synagogues, and meetinghouses sustain community and by sponsoring innovative studies, such as Sacred Places at Risk, that demonstrate the public value of sacred places.

Many of Partners for Sacred Places' services, including a wealth of materials available on the Internet at www.sacredplaces.org, are available free of charge or at a reduced cost to congregations.

Complete Guide to Capital Campaigns for Historic Churches and Synagogues

By Peggy Powell Dean and Susanna A. Jones

Philadelphia: Partners for Sacred Places, 1991; revised edition, 1998.

A comprehensive guide to managing fund-raising campaigns, with step-by-step instructions and innovative strategies for congregations of all sizes. Sample worksheets and letters demonstrate how to broaden the funding focus from the congregation to community members and grant-makers. Available from Partners for Sacred Places. Price: $40 for members of Partners; $50 for nonmembers.

Online Information Clearinghouse

www.sacredplaces.org/info.htm

Partners' unique Information Clearinghouse library is available online. Internet users can browse the clearinghouse database, which serves as an annotated card catalog of the collections, or view and print more than 125 articles on the care and preservation of religious properties. These articles cover a broad range of topics, including fund-raising, stained-glass protection and restoration, energy conservation, architectural history, historic landmark designation, building maintenance, organ restoration, care of graveyards and cemeteries, slate roof repair, project management, adaptive reuse profiles, handicapped accessibility, fire safety, and more.

Sacred Places at Risk

By Diane Cohen and A. Robert Jaeger

Philadelphia: Partners for Sacred Places, 1998.

This important national study provides new evidence about how congregations with historic buildings use their properties for a wide array of community outreach programs. The study also documents the imperiled physical condition of these buildings—and consequently the danger of losing the programs they house. By supplying numbers to support widely known anecdotal evidence, the study presents a strong argument for the sound stewardship of these sacred places. Available from Partners for Sacred Places. Price: $10 for members of Partners; $15 for nonmembers.

Sacred Places in Transition
By A. Robert Jaeger
Philadelphia: Partners for Sacred Places, 1994.
Describes design concepts for three parish properties in Detroit and offers guidelines for communities to plan collaboratively for the future of older and historic religious buildings undergoing changes in use and ownership. Available from Partners for Sacred Places. Price: $10 for members of Partners; $15 for nonmembers.

Strategies for the Stewardship and Active Use of Older and Historic Religious Properties
By Diane Cohen and A. Robert Jaeger
Washington, D.C.: National Trust for Historic Preservation, 1996.
(202) 588-6296
www.preservationbooks.org
A 35-page booklet that provides an overview of the nation's religious landscape, followed by practical assistance on a wide range of topics such as sharing space, building repairs, raising funds, and reuse. Includes a list of helping organizations and published resources. Available from Partners for Sacred Places. Price: $6.

Is It Time to Fold the Tent?
Indianapolis: Christian Church Foundation and the Board of Christian Extension of the Christian Church (Disciples of Christ), n.d.
(317) 635-6500
Workbook helps Disciples of Christ congregations address the issue of whether to close the church doors permanently. For those that do decide to close, the workbook offers step-by-step guidance. Available from the Board of Christian Extension.

Reuse/Shared Use

Amazing Space: Opening Doors to Community Ministry
By Valjean McLenighan
Chicago: Inspired Partnerships, 1994.
(312) 294-0077
Written for clergy and congregational administrators, trustees, and officers, this guide outlines the planning and working process for churches and synagogues sharing space for community ministry. Available from Partners for Sacred Places. Price: $6.

Churches: A Question of Conversion
By Ken Powell and Celia de la Hey
London: SAVE Britain's Heritage, 1987.
www.savebritainsheritage.org
An illustrated book documenting the reuse of vacant or redundant churches; larger preservation questions are discussed as well. Available from www.savebritainsheritage.org/books.htm. Price: £9.95.

Evaluating Your Church Site and Building for Redevelopment
By The Rev. Sherrill Scales, Jr.
New York: Episcopal Church Building Fund, n.d.
(212) 716-6003
www.ecbf.org
Information given on space planning, reconfiguration of internal functions, and the redevelopment and rethinking of properties for congregational uses.

Hints and Guidelines for Calculating the Cost of Renting Space
The Interfaith Coalition on Energy (ICE)
7217 Oak Avenue
Melrose Park, PA 19027-3222
(215) 635-1122
Comprehensive report contains information about insurance, energy costs, sample leases, and more. Available from the Interfaith Coalition on Energy. Price: $5.

Contributors

Jennifer Lynn Baskerville is an Episcopal priest in the diocese of Newark and a historic preservation consultant specializing in religious properties. Currently she is working with other preservationists to create a statewide organization for the care and maintenance of houses of worship in New Jersey.

Lindsay Louise Biddle, a Presbyterian interim pastor from the Twin Cities in Minnesota, has served five congregations and two campus ministries that have closed in recent years. She is especially interested in the effect different types and degrees of transition have on congregations and how those effects vary with the congregation's size.

Cynthia Marie Chapa has lived in Houston, Texas, for 27 years, where she and her husband have raised three children. Since 1983, she has been a German instructor for a local public high school, a community college, Goethe-Institut, and Rice University.

Paul Daniels has a masters degree in church history from Luther Seminary in St. Paul, Minnesota, and archival training from Columbia University and the University of Minnesota. A certified archivist working with Region 3 of the Evangelical Lutheran Church in America, he assists congregations with a wide range of archival and historical projects.

Len Eberhart is an ordained elder in the United Methodist Church. He began serving as superintendent of the Dubuque District of the Iowa Annual Conference in 1997. He has served parishes throughout the Midwest and was manager of the Cokesbury Education Services team in Nashville.

Terry E. Foland is an ordained minister of the Christian Church (Disciples of Christ) and has been a senior consultant with the Alban Institute for 10 years. He has held various middle-judicatory positions for over 20 years and has been consulting with congregations for 32 years. He especially enjoys working with congregations interested in merger.

N. Nelson Granade, Jr., holds degrees from Auburn University and Southern Baptist Theological Seminary in Louisville, and completed a doctor of ministry at Columbia Theological Seminary in Atlanta. He has served four congregations and is currently pastor of First Baptist Church of North Wilkesboro, North Carolina, which is affiliated with the Cooperative Baptist Fellowship.

Lowell L. Hesterman, a retired pastor in the Evangelical Lutheran Church in America, served parishes in Illinois and Ohio before accepting a call to missionary service in Ethiopia. He later worked for the Division for World Mission of the American Lutheran Church and after his retirement served as the first director of Global Health Ministries.

Chris Hobgood is an ordained minister of the Christian Church (Disciples of Christ) with over two decades of service as a congregation pastor and 15 years as executive minister, currently for the Capital Area. He has been a field consultant with the Alban Institute for 15 years. He is author of *The Once and Future Pastor* (Alban, 1998) and *Welcoming Resistance* (Alban, 2001).

Lucy Kolin is a pastor in the Evangelical Lutheran Church in America in the San Francisco Bay area with particular experience working with congregational closings and mergers. She has been in parish ministry for 16 years and serves as adjunct faculty for Pacific Lutheran Theological Seminary in the areas of worship, leadership, and pastoral formation.

Ellen Morseth is a staff mentor at Worshipful-Work: Center for Transforming Religious Leadership, an ecumenical ministry focusing on the integration of spirituality and administration in church governance. Author of several books, her most recent publication is as coauthor of *Selecting Church Leaders: A Practice in Spiritual Discernment* (Alban, 2002).

Partners for Sacred Places was founded in 1989 and is the nation's only nondenominational, nonprofit organization devoted to helping Americans embrace, care for, and make good use of older and historic religious properties. Partners assists people who care for sacred places and promotes understanding of how these places sustain communities.

Tanya Stormo Rasmussen is a graduate of Boston University School of Theology and an ordained elder in the United Methodist Church. She has served congregations in Illinois and Massachusetts and is currently pastor of the International Church of Lund, Sweden. She is particularly interested in ecumenism and church renewal.

Keith Spencer developed a passion for issues related to church viability during his student years at Lutheran Theological Seminary at Gettysburg while working with Dr. Gil Waldkoenig. Married to his college sweetheart, Piper, he lives in Pembroke Pines, Florida, where they raise their three children and he serves as pastor to the wonderful people of Trinity Lutheran Church.

Gil Waldkoenig pays attention to the traditions that inform congregations and their settings. He teaches courses in rural ministry and the church in society at the Lutheran Theological Seminary at Gettysburg and is coauthor of *Cooperating Congregations: Profiles of Mission Strategies* (Alban, 2000).

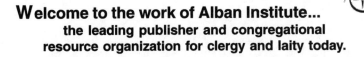

Welcome to the work of Alban Institute...
the leading publisher and congregational resource organization for clergy and laity today.

Your purchase of this book means you have an interest in the kinds of information, research, consulting, networking opportunities and educational seminars that Alban Institute produces and provides. We are a non-denominational, non-profit 25-year-old membership organization dedicated to providing practical and useful support to religious congregations and those who participate in and lead them.

Alban is acknowledged as a pioneer in learning and teaching on *Conflict Management *Faith and Money *Congregational Growth and Change *Leadership Development *Mission and Planning *Clergy Recruitment and Training *Clergy Support, Self-Care and Transition *Spirituality and Faith Development *Congregational Security.

Our membership is comprised of over 8,000 clergy, lay leaders, congregations and institutions who benefit from:
- ❖ 15% discount on hundreds of Alban books
- ❖ $50 per-course tuition discount on education seminars
- ❖ Subscription to *Congregations*, the Alban journal (a $30 value)
- ❖ Access to Alban research and (soon) the "Members-Only" archival section of our web site www.alban.org

For more information on Alban membership or to be added to our catalog mailing list, call 1-800-486-1318, ext.243 or return this form.

Name and Title: _____

Congregation/Organization: _____

Address: _____

City: _____ Tel.: _____

State: _____ Zip: _____ Email: _____

BKIN

The Alban Institute
Attn: Membership Dept.
7315 Wisconsin Avenue
Suite 1250 West
Bethesda, MD 20814-3211